A Theory of Phonological Weight

T0351337

THE DAVID HUME SERIES
PHILOSOPHY AND COGNITIVE SCIENCE REISSUES

The *David Hume Series on Philosophy and Cognitive Science Reissues* consists of previously published works that are important and useful to scholars and students working in the area of cognitive science. The aim of the series is to keep these indispensable works in print.

A THEORY OF PHONOLOGICAL WEIGHT

LARRY M. HYMAN
with a foreword by William R. Leben

THE DAVID HUME SERIES
PHILOSOPHY AND COGNITIVE SCIENCE REISSUES

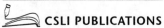 CSLI PUBLICATIONS

Copyright © 2003
CSLI Publications
Center for the Study of Language and Information
Leland Stanford Junior University
Printed in the United States
07 06 05 04 03   5 4 3 2 1

Library of Congress Cataloging-in-Publication Data

Hyman, Larry M.
A theory of phonological weight /
Larry M. Hyman ; with a foreword by William R. Leben.
p.   cm. – (The David Hume series)
Includes bibliographical references and index.

ISBN 1-57586-328-6 (paper : alk. paper)

1. Grammar, Comparative and general–Phonology. 2. Syllabication.
I. Title. II. Series.
P217.3.H94   2003
414—dc21   2003043822
CIP

∞ The acid-free paper used in this book meets the minimum requirements of the
American National Standard for Information Sciences—Permanence of Paper for
Printed Library Materials, ANSI Z39.48-1984.

The David Hume Series of Philosophy and Cognitive Science Reissues consists of previously
published works that are important and useful to scholars and students working in the area of
cognitive science. The aim of the series is to keep these indispensable works in print in affordable
paperback editions.

In addition to this series, CSLI Publications also publishes lecture notes, monographs, working
papers, revised dissertations, and conference proceedings. Our aim is to make new results, ideas,
and approaches available as quickly as possible. Please visit our web site at
http://cslipublications.stanford.edu/
for comments on this and other titles, as well as for changes and corrections by the author and
publisher.

To Lauren

Contents

VIII *Contents*

Introduction to Reissue Edition
William R. Leben and Larry M. Hyman

Larry Hyman's monograph on the mora remains one of the most widely cited works in phonology from the 1980s. At the time it was published, it was the most extensive treatment of the mora that had appeared in print, and the combination of factual coverage from the world's languages and theoretical reasoning about how these facts fit together made for compelling reading. They still do, but the book has been out of print for some time.

CSLI Publications proposed to remedy this problem, and publisher Dikran Karagueuzian suggested adding an introduction, inviting me to divide up the task with author Hyman. As Larry's neighbor on the other side of San Francisco Bay and his friend, colleague, and admirer since grad school days, I jumped at the chance. We decided on an interview format—what better way to address questions that would arise among new and old readers? I hope you'll enjoy the interview and the book.

−WRL

Q: *The mora has been around for a long time. Classical metricians used it to analyze poetry. It has been applied to the analysis of linguistic quantity at least since Trubetzkoy and Jakobson. What was the going view about the mora at the time you decided to write this book?*

A: At the time I wrote my book manuscript, in 1983, the mora was only occasionally mentioned in generative phonology, including non-linear. McCawley (1968) had of course used the mora in his analysis of Japanese, and indeed Japanese remains one of the most prominent languages cited in which moraic structure figures prominently. The mora almost exclusively came up in the analysis of accentual systems, including the "pitch-accent" or "reduced tone" type. Although weight-sensitive stress-accent systems which distinguish heavy vs. light syllables had been analyzed earlier in terms of moras, the generative movement preferred other means. Chomsky & Halle (1968) had, of course, given a strictly segmental analysis of stress attraction to heavy syllables in

English. Even after the syllable was introduced as a prosodic constituent, direct reference to moras was generally avoided. For example, Hayes (1980) defined a heavy syllable as one that has a branching rime (i.e. either a complex nucleus, or a nucleus followed by a coda). At the same time I was working on weight units, Levin [Blevins] (1986) carried this same idea over into her X-bar analysis: a heavy syllable is one that has a branching N or N'. On the other hand, Clements & Keyser (1983), who did not have a rime constituent, had first attempted an analysis defining moras (or contributors to syllable weight) as either a V or C slot that follows a V slot within the syllable. They subsequently introduced a nucleus display which they hypothesized to be maximally binary.

In general, before your book, the mora was regarded as an abstract counting device that measured phonological distance or phonological weight. People counted moras to find the location of stress (and would put the stress on the syllable containing such-and-such a mora), but moras were not themselves feature-bearing units that formed part of a phonological structure. For example, in his 1968 book on Japanese phonology, McCawley famously defined the mora as something that "heavy syllables have two of while light syllables have only one of." But he didn't include moras in phonological representations. Where did your idea of the mora as a structural unit come from?

We have to remember that early generative phonology was very segmentally oriented. Not only did moras not exist as structural units – there weren't syllables either. It wasn't until the post-SPE era, when generative phonology became truly "prosodic", that attention turned on providing constituent-based representations to account for observed generalizations. So, if you had a generalization, you sought an appropriate representation to account for it. In your own work on tone, for instance, you emphasized the suprasegmental properties of tone, and hence had two separate representations. Later Goldsmith (1976) encoded the "semi-autonomy" of tones and segments by means of autosegmental representations.

So now phonological explanations were largely driven by representations: featural tiers, morphemic planes, syllables, feet etc. I had long been interested in the mora, which I had first read about in the Prague School literature – but had been further intrigued by in reading Allen (1973) during my postdoc at Berkeley. Now, in the context of the 1980s, it seemed odd to me that we constantly referred to the notion of "phonological weight" without there being an actual unit of weight. As I recall, I was not attracted to the notion of branchingness – and besides, I concluded that moras could do much more work than distinguish heavy vs. light syllables. As a result, it seemed natural to me to introduce the mora as a constituent, or a structural unit, to use your phrase, to account not only for the distinction between heavy vs. light syllables, but other things as well.

What were the key problems that you intended to solve with the mora?

I started the book with syllable weight because I thought that would be the most accessible. People were already talking about it. More generally than stress, I wanted to provide a representation that would account for the several asymmetries between onsets and codas: (1) onsets do not contribute to the weight of a syllable (codas may); (2) onsets are not tone-bearing units (codas may be); (3) onsets may not be syllabic (codas may be). Concerning this last point, I wish I had had the Ciyao data that we later discovered (Hyman & Ngunga 1997), where we were able to demonstrate, at least for Ciyao, that a CV + syllabic nasal has to be analyzed as a single (bimoraic) syllable. To the above three asymmetries developed in the book, we can add a fourth: (4) onsets do not contribute to compensatory lengthening (codas may), which I mentioned only in passing in my BLS paper (Hyman 1984), influenced by Steriade (1982), but which was developed in great detail in the moraic frameworks of Hock (1986) and Hayes (1989).

What message did you intend by calling your moras "weight units"?

That's an interesting question. Ironically, I remember deciding to use x's instead of μ's, because McCarthy (1981) had already committed μ to stand for "morpheme". By introducing the concept of a "weight unit" (WU), I intended to accomplish two things. First, I could account for weight phenomena. But, second, I intended my x's to be units on what was variously known then as "the skeleton", "the core", "the timing tier", i.e. replacing Clements & Keyser's CV tier, the X's of Levin [Blevins] (1983), the "points" of Kaye and Lowenstamm, etc.

In proposing this replacement, did you see WU's as somehow different from and maybe more appropriate than what these alternatives were able to capture?

I wanted to be able to make direct reference to the units of weight without having to calculate the number of branches, and, rather than a separate moraic plane or display, I wanted to have these units mediate between the higher syllable nodes and the segmental features that were organized beneath them. I had been influenced both by the first draft of what became Clements & Keyser (1983), as well as by Steriade (1982), and was communicating with John McCarthy at the time, who of course had set the scene for all of this work. What I was trying to do was use the structural units for skeletal slots as well as prosodic moras. To do this, I had to start with each (non-geminate) segment having its own WU (x). In the case of /pa/ there would be two input WUs, but the onset-creation rule would remove the x of a [+cons] segment when followed by a [-cons] segment. As a consequence, /pa/ would surface with a single WU, i.e. as a single mora. Thus, as you can see, there were large differences between input vs. output representations, something not surprising, given how derivational most phonology was at the time.

Isn't it interesting that not long after this Itô in her 1986 thesis considered and discarded rule-based systems for building syllable structure? We owe to her the idea that prosodic licensing could distinguish between well-formed and ill-formed segment configurations in syllables. Do you think that your account of moraic structure might lend itself to an analogous structure-licensing rather than structure-building approach?

Itô's dissertation was very elegant and has justifiably had a great influence on all of our thinking. If I were doing things over again today, I would try to minimize the procedural seriality that I adopted in *TPW*.

Clements and Keyser in their 1983 monograph CV Phonology *offer a separate nucleus tier with an element associated with two weight units as a way of representing heavy syllables. Do you have any comment on this kind of representation?*

First, there is the minor question of whether there are trimoraic syllables, and hence, whether their nucleus tier needs to allow for that. It's conceivable that one might try to have a moraic representation on a separate plane. The question is whether Clements and Keyser's υ-display can account for both the above-mentioned as well as other uses of the mora. For example, they would have to stipulate that the delinking of a nuclear C can lead to compensatory lengthening, whereas the delinking of a prenuclear C cannot. Also, there have been proposals where moras exist outside syllables. I'm not only thinking of the Gokana case I described in some detail, but also Bagemihl's (1991) account of such words in Bella Coola as c'ktskʷc' 'he arrived' and t'χt' 'stone'. These words, which lack any sonorant segments (e.g. vowels) are syllable-less. Their segments are moraically licensed. (I could have said the same about Gokana.) Other cases that have been reported are perhaps less extreme, but leave open the possibility of some moras not being incorporated into syllables, e.g. Lin's (1997) account of Piro. Of course, if the υ-display serves as a basis for forming higher prosodic units (as when languages establish bimoraic feet), then it becomes rather equivalent to a moraic projection – in which case one might as well project a μ directly from each moraic segment, as in Zec (1988), Hayes (1989) etc.

Perhaps you're asking whether moras should be represented as structural units or not. It's hard to find good arguments. Although this is a complex matter, there are cases in language games where it is useful to have moras as constituents. Fusa Katada, a student of ours at USC presented a rather nice case in support of the mora from the Japanese language game Shiritori 'hip taking'. In taking turns, each player must advance a word that begins with the same mora with which the last word ends, e.g. *tubame* 'swallow' → *medaka* 'killfish'. That it is the mora that is at play here, and not the syllable, is seen from examples like *budoo* 'grape' → origami (not, for example, *doobutu 'animal'). This seems like a nice argument that speakers are manipulating the mora as a unit. Now of course it could be claimed that you don't really need constituents to do this – and sometimes moras don't help you.

Broselow, in her chapter in the Goldsmith volume The Handbook of Phonological Theory *summarizes and compares current approaches to the mora. She says that you derive moras from units on a timing tier, while Hock (1986) adds an autosegmental moraic level to existing CV skeletal tier, and McCarthy and Prince (1986) and Hayes (1989) replace the skeletal tier with the mora tier. These proposals sound very different. Do you know of any facts or other considerations that recommend one of these views, hopefully your own, against the others?*

Yes, it's true that I derived moras from a "weight tier" in the sense that surviving x's are moras. And yes, it certainly was my intention to replace the CV/X tier with WUs. However, I think one has to distinguish between the different functions of the CV/X tier as it was conceived then. On the one hand, C, V or X units encoded quantity, i.e. whether a consonant or vowel was simple or geminate (or even floating, in case it lacked a skeletal unit). This is the function that was taken over by WUs or moras. However, the second function was that of grouping different feature tiers together to define what was a segment. This function was shortly taken over by the root node in feature geometry (Clements 1985). So, to some extent the C's and V's were replaced by two things: the prosodic mora and the segmental root node. The latter are of course not identical to CV or X slots, but they come close – cf. for example Selkirk's (1990) two-root-node proposal for geminates.

Concerning facts or considerations that may choose between the different views you cite, there have been some attempts to do this, e.g. Tranel (1991), Pulleyblank (1994). But I personally don't think that there has been any "knock-out argument". I think my WUs were found to be cumbersome after simpler moraic representations were introduced, and other questions of representation have, as far as I know, not been fully resolved (e.g. whether the onset should link to a mora, as in my framework, or to the syllable node, as in Hayes'). In reading the different arguments, I sometimes get the feeling that it's six of one and half a dozen of another – and as elsewhere in linguistics, it sometimes comes down to what insights you wish to highlight. Or it may be that we don't have the final answer yet.

The mora obviously has an important role to play in prosodic morphology, as

*shown in even the earliest version of prosodic morphology expounded by Mc-
Carthy and Prince in 1986. Does the mora's role in prosodic morphology tell us
anything more about the mora, beyond what you show in your book?*

I remain very excited about McCarthy & Prince's prosodic morphology, which
has had great influence in the field. The important role that they were able to
ascribe to the mora in reduplication or templatic morphology was additional
evidence of the need to directly incorporate phonological weight into phonological theory. While some of their results bear resemblance to the heavy vs. light
distinction needed for syllable stress, the motivation seemed quite different: A
requirement that a stressed syllable be heavy (bimoraic) can be related to prominence, ultimately phonetic considerations. A requirement that a reduplicant be
bimoraic (even when the base may be monomoraic!) is more mysterious, hence
more interesting. In answer to your question, I felt that McCarthy & Prince vin-
dicated the notion that the mora is a structural unit. Whereas one could identify
a bimoraic template diachronically as a syllable node with a macron ($\bar{\sigma}$), I preferred to think of such a reduplicative template as a branching syllable dominating two moras to which the segmental melody would map.

*Hayes (1989) shows that the mora plays a key role in explaining where compen-
satory lengthening does and does not occur. In your approach, every segment
begins with an underlying mora. Is this model able to distinguish cases that lead
to compensatory lengthening from those that don't?*

Yes, I think so. In my framework, a [+cons] segment automatically became
non-moraic (non-weight-bearing) when followed by a [-cons] segment (vowel).
Unless one were to first have a feature-changing rule, i.e. [+cons] becoming
[-cons], it would take a special statement for the WU of a [+cons] onset to provide the basis for compensatory lengthening. Now everything depends on the
implementation, order of processes, etc.

*Would you be willing to grant that at first glance, an approach which first tried
to identify CV as a moraic unit seems to have more credence, since CV is a surface mora – and an optimal syllable besides?*

Well, I guess I would say CV is a canonical mora – or at least, the canonical initial
mora of a syllable, which in turn should have an onset. But a syllabic nasal, which
is not CV on the surface, is also a mora, as is a vowel that has no onset. Now there
are approaches within government phonology in which the only unit is CV, but
where C or V can be empty. That's a rather abstract approach in which there
would be no structural (hierarchical) difference between mora and syllable.
   Note that everyone has some trouble still with predicting compensatory

lengthening, and whether it is always mora-based has been questioned, most recently by Kavitskaya (2001). Assuming that there is resyllabification, if a bimoraic CVC syllable comes in contact with a following V syllable such that CVC.V → CV.CV, if the second consonant is moraic, it should in principle be possible to get an output CVV.CV. This rarely occurs, however. Typically it is a CVC.CV input that becomes CVV.CV. The best known processes where compensatory lengthening is not conditioned by loss come from the Luganda-style Bantu cases discussed by Clements (1986) and many since (including *TPW*). In these languages, gliding produces length, i.e. CiV → CyVV, and a vowel is lengthened before an NC cluster: CVNCV → CVV.N͡CV. I don't think we yet understand why the latter occurs – or, perhaps rather, if it is so natural, why this phenomenon isn't more widespread outside Bantu. (I'm not convinced that the process doesn't have a Bantu-specific solution, e.g. a *in or *ni origin of moraic nasals, including in class 9/10). Even Kavitskaya seems not to have found CVNCV → CVV.N͡CV outside Bantu (but see Downing 2003).

I should perhaps note that subtle differences in representations have been proposed following instrumental studies of the durational properties of Bantu languages (Maddieson 1993, Hubbard 1995), as well as Arabic dialects (Broselow et al 1997). These authors consider a number of possible relations between segments and their possible representation (e.g. a coda consonant may have its own mora or share one with the preceding vowel; or it may be non-moraic and report directly to the syllable node, etc.). So, rather than worrying about whether my (or some other) framework can capture an opposition, I think we might be concerned to demonstrate whether all of the logical possibilities are in fact attested – and if so, within or across languages?

Does your theory account for the case of Cahuilla brought up by Hayes (1995), which has CVC syllables that are segmentally identical but that differ in length? Hayes accounts for the difference in length by assigning one vs. two moras to the VC rime.

What is difficult about this case is characterizing the morphological process of "intensification" which converts wélnet 'mean one' to wéllnet 'very mean one'. Normally a CVC syllable is light, e.g. [wel] is monomoraic. However, the intensified syllable [wéll] is heavy, i.e. bimoraic. Hayes proposes that intensification be characterized as mora insertion, i.e. [l] is non-moraic (i.e. not subject to his Weight by Position), [ll] is moraic. This is captured very naturally in his system. In mine, I would too would need to insert a WU (because čéxiwèn 'it is clear' becomes čéxxìwen), but this could be accomplished by placing a prosodic requirement on the appropriate syllable – which is construction-specific. Given the meaning of this expressive process, taking a templatic approach does not seem to be an unmotivated move.

Do you see any problems with compensatory lengthening in current thinking, e.g. having to insert a predictable mora for weight-by-position a la Hayes, then reassign it to get CVC.CV → CVV.CV?

This is a very different kind of question from the others, since it is very much dependent on the framework–in two senses. First, it is dependent on the approach taken to moraic representation. In my framework, CVC.CV would of course begin with each segment having a WU. The WU of each prevocalic C would be removed by the onset-creation rule, leaving a bimoraic CVC syllable followed by a monomoraic one. This in turn would be followed by loss of the preconsonantal, followed by spreading of the vowel to the vacated mora. Now, if one followed Hayes (1989) instead, only the two Vs would have an input mora. The preconsonantal C would acquire a mora by "weight by position". Whereas my framework does not require syllabification in order to get a mora on the preconsonantal C, Hayes requires the C to first syllabify as a coda (and acquire its mora), then delink and pass on its mora to the preceding vowel.

Both Hayes and I start with both onset and coda Cs being identical: each has an input WU in my framework, each lacks a mora in Hayes'. Although I need to take a WU away and Hayes needs to insert a mora, the approaches are of equal formal complexity. This is because they are both derivational approaches.

The problem arises in an output-driven approach such as optimality theory (Prince & Smolensky 1993). If Hayes' approach is adopted, a would-be coda C will not have an input mora–since it would predictably acquire one by weight-by-position. The problem is that this isn't the actual output. The preconsonantal C needs to become a coda and then un-become a coda, so to speak. To get this, something additional is required beyond input–output relations, one solution being Sprouse's (1997) "enriched input" idea.

Of course I can't gloat that my framework avoids the problem, since, according to the richness of the base hypothesis, one has to consider both moraic and non-moraic codas in the input–and I of course did not have a way of inserting WUs in a principled way. So, it is as I said: dependent on the framework you adopt and the assumptions that come with it.

Has your work on the mora had any effect on how we view the syllable? Do some of the generalizations previously thought to involve syllables instead flow from your conception of the mora? In your paper on Gokana you went so far as to say that the standard evidences for syllables are lacking, due to the effects of moras. Do you believe that Gokana has syllables?

Well, I would like to think that this work was influential in getting a lot of people to think about the immediate syllable subconstituents as moras. At the time we had so many differents views concerning the internal structure of the syllable.

At one extreme was a completely flat syllable, with no subconstituents, as in Kahn (1976) and Clements & Keyser. C's and V's just reported to sigma. At the other extreme was the view of Cairns & Feinstein (1982), for whom every segment constituted a separate labeled subconstituent. Most views were somewhere in between, but most widespread view was certainly the traditional one (cf. Pike & Pike 1947), that the syllable branches into an onset and a rime (and the latter perhaps in turn into a nucleus and coda). As Levin [Blevins] (1986) codified it, the hierarchical syllable had a right-branching structure (e.g. C-VC). My proposal was that the syllable typically had a left-branching structure (e.g. CV-C). This is another area where I think there is something to be said for the different views.

While the moraic syllable is always mentioned as having a certain attraction, my proposal that the syllable might not be a universal has not, to my knowledge, been met with approval (or much reaction). A veteran and witness of many of the changes that had affected phonological theory (including excesses), although the syllable had previously been maligned in generative phonology, I was struck in the early 1980s by how all was forgiven. Everyone loved the syllable, which was now everywhere in evidence. I wondered if it was being overplayed. A surprising result was that once I introduced WUs or moras into phonological representation, some of the roles of syllables could be reformulated in terms of WUs – which in turn were needed for the skeletal tier.

I had been working for some time on Gokana, a Cross-River language of Nigeria, and had already published an article (Hyman 1983) questioning whether Gokana showed any evidence for syllables at all. Of course it is hard to show that a language lacks something, but none of the typical evidence was there: It is not needed for distributional statements (e.g. Gokana does not have onset-coda asymmetries, rather it has stem-C1 vs. stem-C2 asymmetries) or for phonological rules (which are never syllable-based in Gokana). The syllable is not needed as a TBU – rather, the mora is – and reduplication does not need a syllable template, rather a moraic (CV) one. In my CLS paper (Hyman 1990), I later grudgingly allowed for a stem-initial CV syllable to account for phenomena that are now referred to as initial stem-syllable positional faithfulness (Beckman 1997), but I still basically believe that Gokana prosody is not organized on the basis of syllables.

To show this, I often cite the example aɛ̀ kɔ mm̀ kɛ̀ɛ̀ɛ̀ɛ̀ɛ́'he$_i$ said that I woke him$_i$ up', which I refer to as an "embarras de voyelles". How can six surface WUs of nasalized ɛ (from eight underlying) be syllabified? Nothing depends on it, so we could say that it is done by twos (left-to-right? right-to-left?), or even by ones, each mora being a syllable. Nothing hinges on this. Putting this together with all of the other observations, I concluded that moras (WUs) were all there were!

A few years later Bagemihl (1991) proposed that segments could be "moraically licensed" to account for the "embarras de consonnes" in Bella Coola, some of which are not syllabified. Other also have had moras outside syllables, e.g. Lin's (1997) analysis of Piro. I think that an argument can be made that Matisoff's (1973) Southeast Asian sesquisyllabicity can be regarded as "a mora and a syllable", and so forth. There have been analyses of other phenomena where a layer in the prosodic hierarchy has been skipped. So why not moras that report directly to the prosodic word?

Any comments on Zec's 1988 approach to moraic phonology?

In *TPW* I was aware that there were cases where one would have to put conditions on WUs for the purpose either of syllable weight or tone mapping. That is, not all moras are equal. I liked very much the suggestions in Zec (1988), who, first, distinguished the two moras of a bimoraic syllables as "strong-weak", and, second, placed sonority constraints on the latter. Thus, in some languages, a sonorant coda may be moraic, while an obstruent (e.g. stop) coda may not be. Or, one can restrict tone-bearing units either to [-cons] moras or to [+son] ones. This is useful in many Asian tone systems, where only "smooth" syllables (i.e. open–typically CVV–syllables and syllables closed by a sonorant consonant) can contrast tone. The only use I made of sonority in *TPW* was in defining syllabicity as the most sonorous segment dominated by a mora.

The early 1980s was a period in which numerous proposals were floated that varied in their treatment of syllable sub-constituencies, the skeleton, features, and sonority. To show this in my courses I typically cite the English word "flounce" from Selkirk (1982), showing how different scholars would encode syllabicity.

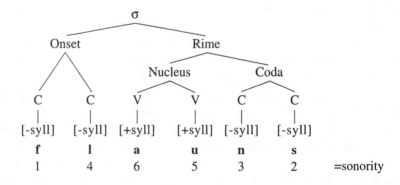

I point out that information about syllabicity can be encoded in any of four different places in the representation: (i) by being in the nucleus; (ii) by having a V slot; (iii) by having a feature specification [+syll]; or (iv) by an intrinsic sonority scale. Recognizing that this is overkill, different scholars proposed streamlining the above representation: Clements & Keyser gave up onset-rime-nucleus (although they did have a nucleus display, as you pointed out); Levin kept a hierarchical representation of the syllable, but gave up CV in favor of X; and so forth.

Can you comment on your proposal that the mora is the TBU in some languages? What does this buy that we cannot have if the syllable (or syllable nucleus) is the TBU? Nancy Woo in her 1969 thesis "Prosody and Phonology" attempted in a rudimentary way to connect tones with weight units by proposing that long vowels were VV sequences and that individual level tones could go each V. This predicted that monomoraic vowels could only have level tones, while VV sequences could also have tones like LH and HL. Taking the mora as the TBU yields the same kind of result. But what does this say about LHL, for example? Can this only occur on a trimoraic syllable?

This is an area of great joy to both of us – predicting tonal behavior. There are many tone languages where tones (tonal melodies) are distributed by moras. Thus, a H-L melody is mapped as H-L-L on trisyllabic CV.CV.CV stems and HL-L on bisyllabic CVV.CV stems in Kukuya (Paulian 1975, Hyman 1987). The same melody is realized H-L on CV.CV stems. So, there is no question that one has to recognize moras – or V slots – in many languages.

Now what you bring up is something different, I think. Since Woo (1969) an idea that just simply won't die is that you can't get contour tones on single moras. Duanmu (1994) has been the most outspoken scholar advocating this view, and it does seem that there is something to it in some Chinese dialects. However, the African experience does not back him up (as he tentatively recognizes in his *LI* article in citing my Kukuya example). There are lots of languages that have contours on short vowels, and although other scholars such as Zhang (2001) and Gordon (2001) note that these vowels may be slightly longer, phonetically, than corresponding vowels realized with level tones, they are still clearly one structural, phonological unit. While I believe that Woo and Duanmu rule out cases of multiple linking of tone to a single mora, we do still have another problem to deal with, which I raised in my *Linguistique Africaine* article (Hyman 1988). Unless there are constraints, a contour such as HL could map one-to-one onto two moras (páà) – or either of the tones could be doubly linked, with the other tone sharing a mora. (pâà, páâ). Occasionally there has been a proposal to recognize two kinds of contours based on the slope, but I have not been able to study these. In any case, I don't believe such oppositions exist – and every case I've known where I have transcribed a CVV with a HL on the first mora and a L on the second, or a H on the first mora and a HL on the second, there has been evidence that we are dealing with two syllables (pâ.à, pá.â). I do not have first-hand experience with LHL and HLH contours on one syllable, but in the same article I suggest that these would be mapped as [păà, pâá], rather than *[pàà, páă] – i.e. the contour would go on the first (strong) mora of the syllable, not on the second, weak mora.

If the mora is a TBU, what does this say about your proposal that underlying every segment is assigned a mora? As Pulleyblank (1994) comments, only certain moras seem to function as TBUs. Does your approach have a way of correctly singling out which ones?

This has bothered me a great deal, and I don't think we've really come to grips with the full significance of Pulleyblank's remarks. For example, melodies: only vowels seem to count; you don't have Mende-style languages that have closed syllables (Kukuya etc.) It would seem that moras are not all equal, that is, that some mora-dependent phenomena sometimes require greater sonority than others (Steriade 1991, Hyman 1992, Gordon 1999, 2002, and others).

Can you tell us whether your work on moraic mismatches changes anything in your original conception of the mora? In English, I can tell you pretty quickly how many syllables most words have, but if you ask me how many moras are in a word like respect, *or* flagellate, *I have to stop and count. Why should this be? Do you think that the situation is different in Gokana?*

Yes, the situation is different in Gokana. The example I cited (kɛ̀ɛ̀ɛ̀ɛ̀ɛ́) can be easily counted in terms of beats, but not syllables – unless one trivially assumed that every beat is a syllable. I assume the situation is different in Bella Coola also.

We often hear of "moraic theory," but I wonder if there really is a theory of moras. For example, Blevins (1995) notes that there are three ways in which languages can define syllable weight. Type 1 languages group count rhymes of the form VV and VC as heavy, with a rhyme consisting of a single V considered light. Type 2 languages count rhymes of the form VV as heavy, while V and VC count as light. Type 3 languages have a three-way weight contrast. V is light, VC is ordinarily heavy, and VV is extra-heavy. Furthermore, which consonants count as moraic differs to some extent from language to language. A theory of all this should distinguish between occurring and non-occurring types and should offer some independent features that follow from membership in one or another type. Is there such a theory?

Zec (1988) tried to do this, and it has been taken up again by Gordon (1999), Morén (1999), and others. One approach is to cite the sonority scale (more sonorous segments tend to be moraic), another is to refer to intrinsic phonetic properties of segments. Some of the results are quite robust (e.g. sonorant codas can be moraic in Lithuanian, while obstruents are not), but this a complicated matter that deserves much further study.

In the light of what you just told me, what is the relevance today of the publication of this reissue of your book?

I'm happy that CSLI Publications has agreed to make this volume available for the new phonology student. I am a firm believer in knowing where we come from, and, like Clements & Keyser (1983), whose first draft was a kind of model for me, I go through all of the reasoning that led to the WU representations. I also leave open a number of issues for further investigation – either in terms of phonological and/or in terms of phonetic consequences of moraic representations. As mentioned, a number of scholars have subsequently become interested in doing instrumental work to test the durational properties of claimed moraic representations (Broselow et al 1997, Gordon 1999, 2002, Hubbard 1995, Maddieson 1993 etc.).

References

Allen, W. Syndey. 1973. *Accent and rhythm. Prosodic features of Latin and Greek: A study in theory and reconstruction*. Cambridge University Press.

Bagemihl, Bruce. 1991. Syllable structure in Bella Coola. *Linguistic Inquiry* 22.589–646.

Beckman, Jill N. 1997. Positional faithfulness, positional neutralisation, and Shona vowel harmony. *Phonology* 14.1–46.

Broselow, Ellen. 1995. Skeletal positions and moras. In John A. Goldsmith (ed.), *The Handbook of Phonological Theory*, 175–205. Cambridge, MA: Blackwell.

Broselow, Ellen, Su-I. Chen and Marie Huffman. 1997. Syllable weight: convergence of phonology and phonetics. *Phonology* 14.47–82.

Cairns, Charles E. & Mark H. Feinstein, M. 1982. Markedness and the theory of syllable structure. *Linguistic Inquiry* 13.193–226.

Chomsky, Noam & Morris Halle. 1968. *The sound pattern of English*. New York: Harper & Row.

Clements, George N. 1986. Compensatory lengthening and consonant gemination in Luganda. In Leo Wetzels & Engin Sezer (eds), *Studies in compensatory lengthening*, 37–77. Dordrecht: Foris.

Clements, George N. & S. Jay Keyser. 1983. *CV phonology*. Cambridge, Mass.: MIT Press.

Downing, Laura J. 2003. On the ambiguous segmental status of nasals in homorganic NC sequences. First Old World Conference on Phonology (OCP 1). University of Leiden, 9–11 January 2003.

Duanmu, San. 1994. Against contour tone units. *Linguistic Inquiry* 25.555–608.

Goldsmith, John. 1976. Autosegmental phonology. Doctoral dissertation, MIT.

Gordon, Matthew. 1999. Syllable weight: phonetics, phonology and typology. Doctoral dissertation, UCLA.

Gordon, Matthew. 2001. A typology of contour tone restrictions. *Studies in Language* 25.405–444.

Gordon, Matthew. 2002. A phonetically-driven account of syllable weight. *Language* 78. 51–80.

Hayes, Bruce. 1981. A metrical theory of stress rules. Doctoral dissertation, MIT.

Hayes, Bruce. 1989. Compensatory lengthening in moraic phonology. *Linguistic Inquiry* 20.253–306.

Hayes, Bruce. 1995. *Metrical stress theory: Principles and case studies*. Chicago: University of Chicago Press.

Hubbard, Kathleen. 1995. "Prenasalized consonants" and syllable timing: evidence from Runyambo and Luganda. *Phonology* 235.256.

Hock, Hans. 1986. Compensatory lengthening: In defense of the concept "mora". *Folia Linguistica* 20.431–460.

Hyman, Larry M. 1983. Are there syllables in Gokana? In J. Kaye et al (eds), *Current approaches to African linguistics*, vol. 2. Dordrecht: Foris. 171–179.

Hyman, Larry M. 1984. On the weightlessness of syllable onsets. In *Proceedings of the 10th Annual Meeting of the Berkeley Linguistic Society*, 1–14.

Hyman, Larry M. 1987. Prosodic domains in Kukuya. *Natural Language and Linguistic Theory* 5.311–333.

Hyman, Larry M. 1988. Syllable structure constraints on tonal contours. *Linguistique Africaine* 1.49–60.

Hyman, Larry M. 1990. Non-exhaustive syllabification: evidence from Nigeria and Cameroon. In *Papers from the Parasession on the Syllable in Phonetics and Phonology*. Chicago Linguistic Society 26.175–195.

Hyman, Larry M. 1992. Moraic mismatches in Bantu. *Phonology* 9.255–265.

Hyman, Larry M. & Armindo Ngunga. 1997. "Two kinds of moraic nasal in Ciyao". *Studies in African Linguistics* 26.131–163.

Ito, Junko. 1986. Syllable theory in prosodic phonology. Ph.D. Dissertation. G.S.L.A. University of Massachusetts, Amherst.

Kahn, Daniel. 1976. Syllable-based generalizations in English phonology. Ph.D. Dissertation, M.I.T.

Katada, F. 1990. On the Representaion of Moras: Evidence from a Language Game. *Linguistic Inquiry* 21.4:641–646.

Kavitskaya, Daria. 2001. Compensatory lengtheing: phonetics, phonology, diachrony. Doctoral dissertation, University of California, Berkeley (to appear, Routledge).

Kaye, Jonathan & Jean Lowenstamm. 1984. De la syllabicité. In François Dell, Daniel Hirst & Jean-Roger Vergnaud (eds), *Forme sonore du langage*, 123–160. Paris: Hermann.

Levin [Blevins], Juliette. 1983. Reduplication and prosodic structure. Ms. MIT.

Levin [Blevins], Juliette. 1985. A metrical theory of syllabicity. Doctoral dissertation, MIT.

Lin, Yen-Hwei. 1997. Syllabic and moraic structures in Piro. *Phonology* 14.403–436.

Maddieson, Ian. 1993. Splitting the mora. UCLA Working Papers in Phonetics 83.9–18.

Matisoff, James A. 1973. Tonogenesis in Southeast Asia. In Larry M. Hyman (ed.), *Consonant types and tone*, 71–95. Southern California Occasional Papers in Linguistics 1. Los Angeles: University of Southern California.

McCarthy, John J. 1981. A prosodic theory of nonconcatenative morphology. *Linguistic Inquiry* 12.373–418.

McCarthy, John & Alan Prince. 1986. Prosodic morphology. Ms. Excerpted in John A. Goldsmith (ed.), *Phonological theory: the essential readings*, 238–288. Malden, MA: Blackwell.

McCawley, James D. 1968. *The phonological component of a grammar of Japanese*. Monographs on Linguistic Analysis 2. The Hague: Mouton.

Morén, Bruce. 1999. Distinctiveness, Coercion and Sonority: A Unified Theory of Weight. Doctoral dissertation, University of Maryland. ROA #346-0999.

Paulian, Christiane. 1975. *Le kukuya, langue teke du Congo: phonologie, classes nominales.* Paris: Société d'Etudes Linguistiques et Anthropologiques de France.

Pike, Kenneth L. & Eunice V. Pike 1947. Immediate constituents of Mazateco syllables. *International Journal of American Linguistics* 13.78–91.

Pulleyblank, Douglas. 1994. Underlying Mora Structure. *Linguistic Inquiry* 25.344–53

Selkirk, Elisabeth O. 1982. Syllables. In Harry van der Hulst & Norval Smith (eds), *The structure of phonological representations*, vol. 2, 337–383. Dordrecht: Foris.

Selkirk, Elisabeth O. 1990. A two root theory of length. *University of Massachusetts Occasional Papers in Linguistics* 123–171.

Sprouse, Ronald. 1997. A case for enriched inputs. Paper presented at TREND meeting, UC Santa Cruz, May 3, 1997. ROA #193–0597.

Steriade, Donca. 1982. *Greek prosodies and the nature of syllabification.* Doctoral dissertation, MIT.

Steriade, Donca. 1991. Moras and other slots. In D. Meyer & S. Tomioka (eds), *Proceedings of the 1st Meeting of the Formal Linguistics Society of the Midwest.* University of Wisconsin, Madison.

Tranel, Bernard. 1991. CVC light syllables, geminates and moraic theory. *Phonology* 8.291–302.

Woo, Nancy. 1969. Prosody and phonology. Doctoral dissertation, MIT.

Zec, Draga. 1988. Sonority constraints on prosodic structure. Doctoral dissertation, Stanford University.

Zhang, Jie. 2001. The effects of duration and sonority on contour tone distribution: Typological survey and formal analysis. Doctoral disseration, UCLA.

Introduction

All current theories of phonology assume the correctness and adequacy of the syllable as a unit of hierarchical structure. Within these theories the syllable constitutes the lowest unit within a prosodic hierarchy which includes at progressively higher levels the foot, the phonological word, and the phonological phrase (cf. Selkirk 1980, Pike 1967). Phonologists differ, however, in how they represent the internal structure of the syllable. Most phonologists, following Pike and Pike (1947), view the syllable as a branching structure consisting of an onset and a rime (=core) and the rime as consisting of a nucleus (=peak) and a margin (=coda). See, for example, Halle and Vergnaud (1980), Kaye and Lowenstamm (1981), Anderson (1982a) and Steriade (1982), among others. More detailed branching structures are postulated by Kiparsky (1979), who extends the metrical labels *s* and *w* to capture relative degrees of sonority within the syllable, and by Cairns and Feinstein (1982), who argue that both the onset and the margin need to be further broken down into subconstituents. The resulting highly articulated syllable structure differs markedly from the one assumed by Clements and Keyser (1981, 1983), who present a flat three-tiered autosegmental model of the syllable which, for them, has no internal hierarchical structure.

The arguments for the syllable have thus been of two types. First, it has been demonstrated that the syllable is a significant unit in the establishment of higher level prosodic units. The syllable is the typical stress-bearing unit and as such serves as the starting point for the construction of stress-feet (Liberman and Prince 1977, Selkirk 1980, Hayes 1981) and phonological phrases. At the same time, the syllable is a significant unit in determining how lower level segmental units group themselves into constituents. This is particularly clear in the case of consonant clusters which may or may not belong to the same constituent.

* Earlier versions of this paper were presented at the University of California at Berkely, the University of California at Los Angeles, and the University of Southern California. I would like to thank Joseph Aoun, Susan Foster, Bruce Hayes, Juliette Leven, David Pesetsky, Annie Rialland, Ian Roberts, Donca Steriade, and Bernard Tranel for their helpful comments and reactions.

Thus, a sequence VCCV may be syllabified as VC.CV, i.e. a VC syllable followed by a CV syllable, or as V.CCV, i.e. a V syllable followed by a CCV syllable. It may not, on the other hand, be syllabified as *VCC.V, i.e. as a consonant-final syllable followed by a vowel-initial syllable. In order to prevent this kind of syllabification, the numerous syllabic frameworks have invoked principles that automatically result in a CV sequence being assigned to the same syllable.[1] The fact that some languages provide different syllabifications of VCCV according to the nature of the consonants, e.g. according to a sonority hierarchy, provides evidence for the reality of syllable structure. It is not surprising, then, that almost all arguments for the syllable have had to do with problems arising from the analysis of consonant sequences.[2]

The corresponding issue of vowel sequences potentially bears on the question of syllable structure, although in practice there have been few cases where a clear argument has been made (see, however, Kaye 1981). The problem of vowel sequences is inseparable from the problem of analyzing diphthongs. A sequence ai, for instance, has at least three possible representations in most current theories of phonology: a.i (two V's two separate syllables), ai (two V's one syllable), and ai (one complex V, one syllable). (I am assuming in all three cases that we are not dealing with a vowel + glide sequence.) The opposition of relevance in the setting up of syllables is that between V.V and VV. i.e. the first and second representations. As one looks at such possible oppositions it usually turns out to be the case that, if found within the same language, VV belongs to one morpheme, while V.V belongs to two morphemes, e.g. in Kimatuumbi (Odden, n.d.). In addition, if the vowels in question are identical in quality, VV may have a single set of segmental features associated to the two V slots on the CV tier (see below), while V.V may simply be two sets of identical segmental features associated to the successive V's (see Hyman 1982a), which of course belong to different morphemes, as we have said. In this case, the argument for setting up independent syllables for each successive V is less clear – and seems arbitrary in languages where multiple V's of identical quality can appear in sequence. As I argued in the above cited work (cf. also section 3 below), the Gokana language spoken in Eastern Nigeria permits at least up to six identical vowel lengths in sequence, which, it was claimed, are left unsyllabified. It may possibly be the case, as I shall argue further below, that some languages do not have phonological syllables at all and, therefore, that syllabicity (to be defined) may be acquired without syllables.

If this last point turns out to be correct, then the whole of prosodic phonology needs to be reexamined. Despite the differences between the various syllabic frameworks developed recently, most phonologists share the view that the syllable is the lowest unit of hierarchical structure grouping all segments into prosodic categories. In other words, there is no hierarchical unit mediating between the segmental features (whether auto-segmentalized or not) and the syllable.[3]

In the present work I shall present a different view. I shall argue in subsequent sections that as a prior necessary step to syllabification, languages group segments into beats or "weight units" (WU's) which, to some extent, correspond to the traditional notion of the "mora" in certain of its realizations. This proposal is incompatible with the branching syllable structure and, as will be seen, there is no onset/rime opposition in this framework. The grouping of segments into weight units makes different predictions about prosodic structure from either the CV tier or the onset–rime approach to syllabification. I will show in this study that these predictions are borne out and that certain phonological universals can only be captured within the WU framework. In the first section I begin with an examination of the concept of syllable weight. This is followed by a second section introducing the "weight tier" and a third section defining the notion of syllabicity and establishing its logical independence from syllable structure. Subsequent sections demonstrate that what I shall refer to as "WU phonology" in contrast to "CV phonology" is better equipped to capture the properties of syllabic consonants and epenthesis and that a revised view of the nature of glides is required. Finally, I turn to the nature of phonological representations in this theory and present some further thoughts on the feature [cons] and phonetic realization rules to conclude the work.

Chapter 1

Syllable Weight

The distinction between "heavy" and "light" syllables has received considerable attention in recent work. It has been demonstrated in a number of ways that languages may treat some syllable structures as having greater quantity or weight than others (see Newman 1972 for a general statement). Jakobson (1931, 1937) and Trubetzkoy (1939) both note the importance of the syllable weight concept in determining the placement of stress in different languages, something which is taken up also by Allen (1973), Hyman (1977), de Chene (1979), Ohsiek (1978) and others.

Briefly, languages recognizing a heavy vs. light syllable distinction follow one of two patterns:

(a) A first group of languages treats a syllable whose rime consists solely of a short (or lax) vowel as light, whereas a syllable whose rime has either a long (or tense) vowel and/or a final consonant (or more) is treated as heavy. Schematically, a -V rime defines a light syllable and either a -V: or a -VC rime defines a heavy syllable. Well-known cases of this type are Latin, most dialects of Arabic, and, to some extent, English, which skip over a light penultimate syllable to assign antepenultimate stress, for instance. A less well-known example comes from the Hokan language Yana whose stress "...tends to fall on the first heavy syllable, that is, on the first syllable which is either closed with a consonant or which contains a vowel cluster" (Sapir and Swadesh 1960:4). In case there is no such heavy syllable in a word, "...the first syllable tends to carry the stress". Numerous languages are reported to have redundant or "non-phonemic" stress on every such heavy syllable, e.g. Cayapa (Lindskog and Brend 1962:39), Cuna (Holmer 1947:23) and Goajiro (Arawak) (Holmer 1949:50), attesting to the perceptual prominence of -V: and -VC rimes within heavy syllables.

(b) The second group of languages treats a syllable whose rime has a short (or lax) vowel as light and a syllable whose rime has a long (or tense) vowel as heavy - but, independently of whether the syllable is closed by a consonant or not. Schematically, a $-VC_0$ rime defines a light syllable, while a $-V:C_0$ rime defines a heavy syllable. The crucial difference between group (a) and group (b) is, then, that the latter treats a closed syllable with short (or lax) vowel as light, whereas the former treats it as heavy. Languages having this property include Huasteco (Larsen and Pike 1949:269), which places stress on the last long vowel syllable of the word, otherwise on the first syllable, if the word has no long vowel; and Khalka Mongolian (Poppe 1951), which places stress on the first long vowel syllable of the word, otherwise on the first syllable if the word has no long vowel.

No language has been found, to my knowledge, which treats a -VC rime as heavy, but a -V: rime as light. In addition, although a language lacking -VC rimes may treat -V: as heavy and -V as light (e.g. Maori (Hohepa 1967: 10)), no language lacking -VV rimes but having -VC rimes treats the latter as heavy. In other words, as pointed out by Trubetzkoy (1939), in order for a -VC rime to be counted as heavy, the language must also have -V: rimes. Syllable weight is thus necessarily tied to the existence of a vowel length (or vowel tenseness) opposition.[4] This generalization and the parametrization of the -VC rime as heavy or light must therefore be accounted for in an adequate theory of syllable weight.

As indicated in the above summary, the weight of a syllable depends solely on the properties of its rime. All studies on syllable weight thus point out that the number or nature of segments within the syllable onset has no bearing on the weight of the syllable as a whole. A syllable having a CCCV shape, where the V is short or lax, would therefore be a light syllable, even though it consists of four segments. Any account of syllable weight will have to explain also why the onset is "weightless", while the margin may, in some languages, contribute to the weight of the syllable.

In traditional accounts of syllable weight no attempt was made to provide a formal representation of the heavy vs. light distinction. It was essentially stipulated that (a) the onset did not count; and (b) the rime had to have such and such a structure in order to qualify its syllable as heavy. Recently proposals have been made to capture syllable weight in terms of the geometry of the syllable coupled with the notion of a "projection" (Halle and Vergnaud 1980). The three kinds of syllable structures under discussion have the following representations in (1).

(1)   a.   b.   c.

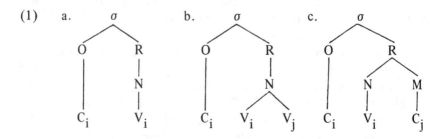

A light syllable (1a) consists of a possible onset (O), which is irrelevant for establishing syllable weight, and a rime (R) consisting solely of a nucleus (N) dominating a single vowel (V). In (1a) this V_i represents a short or lax vowel. In (1b), following Leben (1980) and others, a long or tense vowel is represented as a branching nucleus, which is dominated by the rime node. I have indicated the two vowel units as V_i and V_j, although in the case of a long vowel (as opposed to a sequence of unlike vowels), the two may be identical. There is thus an equivalence between a long or tense vowel and a vowel sequence or diphthong within the same syllable. Finally, in (1c), it is observed that the CVC syllable contains the additional consonant in the margin (M), which closes that syllable. Languages of group (a) thus treat (1b) and (1c) as heavy, while languages of group (b) treat only (1b) as heavy.

Based on the representations in (1), McCarthy (1979) and Hayes (1981), among others, define a light syllable as one whose rime does not branch, and a heavy syllable as one whose rime does branch. Thus, in order to establish the weight of a syllable, only its rime is "projected" and the heavy vs. light distinction is redefined as one between branching vs. non-branching. No explanation for the weightlessness of the onset is provided other than that it is not projected. Hence, a branching onset will not be considered in establishing syllable (here, rime) weight.

While the non-projection of the onset is simply the formal correlate to the traditional exclusion of the onset in calculating weight, one might ask how it is that the notion "branching rime" can be defined either as a true branching rime (1c) *or* as a branching nucleus dominated by a non-branching rime (1b). The branching character of the rime is thus determined at two different levels. Structures such as in (2) also have "branching rimes", if one carries the branching down one level further:

(2)   a.   b.

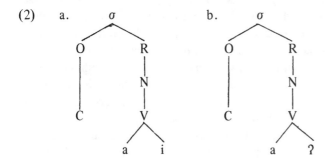

In (2a) there is a single "V slot" on the CV tier (see section 2) which dominates two sets of vowel features, as would be the case of a short diphthong, for instance. Anderson (1984) discusses such a case in Icelandic and other cases of "loose" vs. "close" contact which might be analyzed as the difference between a branching vs. non-branching rime. The representation in (2b) is identical to that in (2a) except that the second set of features dominated by the V is a glottal stop. This might be the representation given to Cayapa CV? syllables which exceptionally are light, whereas other CVC syllables are heavy (Lindskoog and Brend 1962:39). A similar structure was provided by Safir (1979:96) for Capanahua, where CV? does not count as a closed syllable (cf. note 4). It would seem then that if it is the V under the N node that branches, this does not constitute a branching rime; hence, we do not have a heavy syllable, according to this theory. But why should the branching criterion be allowed to apply to the N node, but not one level down to the V slot? Finally, assuming that the correct notion of heaviness is "branching rime", why is it the case that some languages treat (1b) as heavy, but (1c) as light, when the level at which the branching takes place is more deeply embedded in the former than in the latter? It would seem that heaviness is in some sense first a quality of vowels (or [+syll] units), but only secondarily a quality of (some) consonants in the rime.

A major difficulty with the branching rime hypothesis is that additional information is sometimes relevant for the projection. I have mentioned that the glottal stop must not be projected in Cayapa. Similarly, in Chitimacha, where -əC rimes do not make their syllable heavy, but other -VC rimes do (Swadesh 1934:351), the schwa will have to be excluded from the projection. In Dagur Mongolian (Austin 1952:68), the only consonant in a -VC rime which creates a heavy syllable is [ŋ] (which Martin 1961:15 treats as [+syll]). And, finally, many languages have a full/reduced vowel opposition rather than a long/short (or even tense/lax) one. Thus, in Chuvash (Krueger 1961:86), stress goes on the last full vowel of the word or, if there is no full vowel, on the first vowel of the word. Somehow the two reduced vowels /ĕ/ and /ă/ must not be projected, and yet it would be undesirable to have to represent all full vowels as double and the two reduced vowels as single. While there may be ways to reinterpret these and other "exceptions" to the projection (e.g. try to make the schwa epenthetic in Chitimacha, the nasal dominated by a V in Dagur Mongolian, and the glottal stop part of the vowel nucleus in (2b) in Cayapa), such moves strongly suggest that the geometry of the rime is not relevant to syllable weight phenomena.

At least one view of the syllable makes this claim directly. Clements and Keyser (1981, 1983) propose a flat syllable structure yielding the following representations corresponding to those of the branching syllable in (1).

(3) a.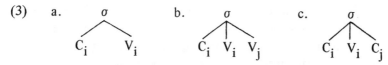

In their view the syllable is represented as an autosegmental tier without internal constituent structure. In their earlier study, Clements and Keyser claim that they can capture the same generlizations about syllable–linked phenomena with a flat syllable as others capture with the branching syllable. For example, a light syllable is defined as one which has as its right-most element a single V, as in (3a). A heavy syllable, on the other hand, is one which either has more than one V, as in (3b), or which has a single V (or more) followed by one or more C's, as in (3c). In other words, a heavy syllable is one that has some element, whether a V or a C, following the *first* V of the syllable. This is reflected more formally in their later study, which sets up a "nucleus display" to account for syllable weight. These accounts essentially recapitulate Jakobson's and Trubetzkoy's notions in that everything is counted except the material preceding the nuclear (=first) vowel.

This account cannot be regarded as an "explanation" of syllable weight, only a recasting of the non-formal account. It has the same problems associated with the exceptional behavior of certain elements of the rime in the languages cited in the previous paragraphs. In fact, in either approach one needs two bits of information: (a) what part of the syllable does the projection scan (answer: it universally ignores the onset); and (b) what elements of the scanned projection are actually projected (e.g. [+full vowels], [-glottal], [+syll] etc., as the case may be).

Once we ignore the geometry (other than the onset–rime distinction, however that distinction is to be represented), we are left with a projection that is very similar, if not identical to projections taken for other purposes. In particular, it is striking that tone languages typically project units of the rime for establishing the tone bearing units and, as in the case of syllable weight, there is some variation in what can carry tone in a given language. In most tone languages only a vowel or syllabic consonant (e.g. syllabic nasal) can carry tone. In other tone (or tonal accent) languages, e.g. Lithuanian (Kenstowicz 1970), any [+son] segment within the rime may carry tone. In still other languages, e.g. Hausa, any segment within the rime, whether sonorant or obstruent, may carry tone. It seems like there is a non–arbitrary relationship between the units which contribute to syllable weight and the units which can carry tone in a language, and yet there is nothing in the projection approach that would make this prediction.

In the preceding discussion we have established that certain segments within the rime contribute to the weight of a syllable. These "weight bearing units" have traditionally been termed "moras" (less technically, beats or timing units). The mora has been invoked more recently in McCawley's (1970) study of Japanese and by de Chene (1979) in his comprehensive study of vowel length. Briefly, a heavy syllable is said to consist of two moras and a light syllable of one. Thus, CV: is treated as CV-V and CVC as CV-C, while CV is treated as a single CV mora. Syllables with more than two moras (e.g. CV-V-C, CV-C-C, etc.) are sometimes referred to as "superheavy", and occur, for example, in Arabic (McCarthy 1979, Aoun 1979). Implicit in this approach to syllable weight is that we do not project only segments within the rime, but rather *all* segments belong to one mora or another.

Now the same moras or beats are typically called upon by tone languages to carry tone. There is, in fact, a strong claim one might make to the effect that a language may not differ in the units it calls upon to establish syllable weight vs. those it calls upon to carry tone (see, however, section 7 for a refinement of this claim). Tone is, as we know, sensitive to the number of units that may be available to carry it. Thus, there are numerous tone languages which may not assign more than one tone to a single tone bearing unit (e.g. vowel), i.e. they may not have tonal contours on a single segment. In most tone and tonal accent languages, it is the mora that is the tone-bearing unit (TBU). Thus, consider the Gokana verb form in (4).

(4)   o   teer-a-i [ò téèràì] 'you pl. run'
       | | \|/
       L   H L

The verb form 'run' (zero tense) has a HL melody which is mapped with the H being assigned to the first vowel and the L being assigned to all successive vowels. Stated as I have just done in terms of vowels, the TBU's are e-e-a-i. Stated in terms of moras, the TBU's are te-e-ra-i. Within the current theory we are forced to project only the vowels, since we have no way of projecting moras, which in all of the syllabic frameworks have no formal existence. If a segment is projected it will count as a TBU. There is thus no way to project two segments as one TBU as would be done in the traditional account.

In Hyman (1983a) it was claimed that Gokana does not have phonological syllables, an issue that will be returned to in section 3. What it means for the present discussion is that we cannot define TBU's in that language in terms of rimes, since rimes do not exist. Yet all approaches to syllable weight and moras have in common that weight is defined as a property of syllables, rather than as an independent property derived, as I shall propose, from the nature of segmental features such as [cons] and [son]. In other words, syllable structure needs to be defined prior to the determination of moras, rather than the reverse. Consider the Lithuanian situation, for example, as described by Kenstowicz (1970). In this language all [+son] segments within the rime (predetermined!) are tone-bearing, i.e. capable of taking a H tone. Not tone bearing are (a) sonorants which are in the onset; or (b) obstruents which are in the onset *or* rime. Because of this distribution, a rising (LH) or falling (HL) tonal contour will be possible only on a CV[+son] syllable. CV and CV[-son] syllables can have only H or L tone. Thus, with respect to tone at least, we would like to say that the onset does not have weight and, also, that an obstruent within the rime does not have weight. In other words, a CV[+son] syllable consists of the two moras CV- and -[+son] (either a vowel or a sonorant consonant), while a CV or CV[-son] consists of a single mora.

The following empirical question must be posed: can a language like Lithuanian have two different projections for establishing syllable weight, on the one hand, and tone-bearing units on the other? In the current theory there is nothing to stop Lithuanian from counting $-V{\left[\substack{-\text{son} \\ C}\right]}$ as two units in establishing syllable weight, for instance, but as one in assigning H tone. The above question immediately arises in the theory of phonological weight to be developed in this study, but will have to be postponed until section 7. For present purposes let us assume the strongest possible position: the units relevant for establishing syllable weight are identical in any language to those relevant for assigning tone. This being assumed, then, how should this relationship be captured formally? I see at least three plausible alternatives:

(a) The first alternative would simply stipulate that there is a single projection for all weight-related phenomena. This would include tone, which is necessarily weight-related, but it might not include, say, harmony processes involving vowel features or nasality. These latter processes would or could have their own distinct projection. In some languages everything within the rime would be projected as weight-bearing; in other languages only [+son] segments within the rime would be projected as weight-bearing; and in still other languages only [+syll] segments (which are necessarily within the rime - but cf. section 4) would be projected. Or, stated somewhat differently, the first language would project everything dominated by the rime node, the third language everything dominated by the nucleus node, and the second language would either assign all of its [+son] segments within the rime to the nucleus (essentially treating nasals, liquids and glides as syllabic), then projecting the nucleus; or it would simply place a restriction that the elements of the rime to be projected must be [+son]. This being permitted, other stipulations could be added, as needed. An evaluation metric would be responsible for measuring how highly valued a particular projection is for a particular purpose - and ultimately, if allowed, how non-highly valued it would be for a language to require two distinct projections for different weight-related phenomena (e.g. syllable weight vs. tone). Given that some of Newman's (1972) syllable-weight phenomena in Chadic languages had to do with tone, it would be surprising if such a state of affairs were to obtain, but, if found, there would be a way to do it (two separate projections) in this approach.

(b) An alternative might be to propose a phonological feature of weight, say [+W], which could exist on a separate tier much like tonal features or nasality. The onsets would then be characterized as "opaque" in the sense of Clements (1981) and Clements and Sezer (1983): any segment within the onset would be [-W] and other segments would be [+W] or [-W] depending on the language. In this approach we define what can be a "weight bearing unit", which unit is then available for any and all feature associations having to do with weight, e.g. tone. Like the preceding suggestion, this approach would require syllable formation to precede the establishment of weight units, even in languages where all [+syll] segments are tone-bearing and are identifiable without syllable structure. Since this feature would be derived from other features such as [syll], [son] and [cons], it would seem to be an unnecessarily redundant one, and we could refer directly to these features.

(c) The third approach, which will be argued in the following section, is for there to be a central "weight tier" where weight is represented directly. This tier, which replaces the CV tier of other models, consists solely of weight units (WU's), indicated by an x, which mediate between the different autosegmental tiers and which serve as the input to syllable formation in languages having syllable structure. In other words, if it can be demonstrated that there is a single tier to receive tonal features and to serve as input to syllabification, the problem of having a single weight projection will have been solved. In fact, I will attempt to show that most (all?) projections can be eliminated if such a tier is adopted.

Chapter 2

The Weight Tier

Before addressing the proposed weight tier, let us consider the CV tier or core of most current phonological models. This tier has three basic functions:

(a) It provides the value of syllabicity for segmental matrices, since C = [–syll] and V = [+syll] (McCarthy 1979, 1981).

(b) It provides a measure of the "number of units" present of each segmental matrix.

(c) It provides for most phonologists (but not all; see McCarthy 1983a) the core through which autosegmental tiers and prosodic structure connect.

Let us briefly consider each of these. First, the CV tier provides the value of the feature [syll]. This is the least important function of the CV tier since there are other ways of predicting syllabicity. For example, if there is a branching syllable structure, it will generally have enough information in itself to predict that both the onset and margin dominate [–syll] segments and the nucleus dominates [+syll] segments. Or, in addition to or instead of the branching syllable structure, the value of the feature [syll] can be largely predicted from the other features of the segmental matrices, particularly the features [cons] and [son]. The possible problems in attempting to define syllabicity in this way involve syllabic consonants and non–syllabic vowels (i.e. glides), whose analysis is addressed in sections 4 and 6, respectively. To a very great extent, then, this first function of the CV tier can be replaced by either syllable structure and/or direct reference to other segmental features.

The second function has to do with the number of units each set of segmental matrices is associated with. There appear to be only three possiblities, shown first for C's in (5).

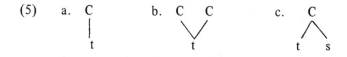

(5) a. C   b. C   C   c. C
         | \   /   / \
         t   t   t   s

The most common situation is for one [+cons] set of features to be associated with a single C slot as in (5a). However, as shown by Schein

(1981) for Tigrinya, a geminate consonant may require the representation
in (5b), where a single [+cons] matrix is associated with two C slots.
This representation is distinct from a sequence of one-to-one associations,
i.e. two C's each with its own identical [+cons] matrix. As stated above
for vowels, a sequence of representations such as in (5a) would be possible only if each C with its feature matrix belongs to a separate morpheme.
Finally, as seen in (5c), two feature matrices (or, conceivably, partial
feature matrices) may be associated with a single C slot, in which case
we obtain a complex consonant segment. The example shown is the affricate t[s], though parallel representations may be provided to prenasalized
consonants, consonants with palatal or labial offglides etc.

The same three-way distinction is necessary with respect to vowels,
as seen in (6).

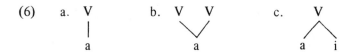

In (6a) we see the most frequently attested association: one [-cons]
matrix is associated with one V slot. In (6b) the representation of a
geminate vowel is given which, as demonstrated by Hyman (1982a)
for Gokana, is distinct from two identical instances of (6a) in sequence.
Finally, in (6c) the possibility of a short dipthong is given, where neither
[-cons] matrix is a glide.

It is clear that we need some way to represent both geminate or double
associations of a single feature matrix, as well as associations of two feature matrices with a single slot on the CV tier. However, we need not assume C and V entities for this purpose. In my 1982a study of Gokana,
for instance, I argued for a tier of x's representing [+seg] was sufficient
without a feature [syll] for capturing the generalizations of segment syllabicity and length in that language (cf. section 3). In other words, we
have the representations in (5′) and (6′).

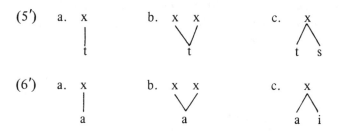

This x-tier, where each x = [+seg], does not distinguish between weight-bearing and non-weight-bearing segments; it merely points out how many "lengths" there are of each feature matrix.

The final function of the CV tier is to serve as a core for the different segmental and autosegmentalized features to attach to, as well as for the construction of syllables or, in the absence of syllables, of other prosodic units (e.g. the foot or the phonological word). Most phonologists seem to accept that this tier has a special status. Instead of tiers relating in all possible ways to each other, they are connected by mediation of the CV tier. McCarthy (1983a) has a different type of tier-connection, and it may be that some relationships between morphological tiers need a different kind of representation. This raises the possibility that the tier itself may be a morpheme, as in the CV-templates or skeleta which McCarthy (1981) assumes for the binyanim of Arabic. However, as will be addressed in section 7, the theory developed here forces a reinterpretation of his C's and V's as x's with "pre-associated" values of the feature [cons].

In what follows I shall take the position that syllabicity need not be represented directly on the CV tier. Thus the first function of the CV tier is rejected. The second and third functions are accepted as proper functions of the x-tier which results from eliminating the feature [syll] from the CV tier. However, I shall reinterpret the x-tier so that instead of being a sequence of [+seg] units, these x's are representations of *phonological weight*. They are weight units (WU's) which will be available for the two functions we retain of the CV tier.

In this reinterpretation of the CV-tier and other slot- or [+seg]-based conceptions of the core (see, for instance, Kaye and Lowenstamm 1981, Hyman 1982a, and, more recently, Levin 1983 and McCarthy 1983b), we retain representations such as in (5′) and (6′). Underlyingly each segmental matrix of features will be associated with one or two x's and may be coassociated with another segmental matrix to produce the complex segments in (5′c) and (6′c). We also will allow, discussed in section 5, a segmental matrix to exist without an x, i.e. to be a "floating segment". This is the analysis of the "silent" final consonants of French, as in petit [pəti] 'little (m.)', whose second /t/ has no x and hence cannot be pronounced unless an x follows for it to attach to (see below).

The underlying x-associations will be modified by both universal and language-specific rules. The most important such rule is the onset-creation rule (OCR) provided in (7).

(7)

$$[\text{+cons}] \qquad [\text{-cons}]$$

e.g.

$$t \qquad a$$

The OCR in (7) states that whenever a [+cons] segment is followed by a [-cons] segment, the WU of the former is deleted (symbolized by the circle around the x), and the [+cons] feature matrix associates to the x of the [-cons] matrix to the right. As a result, two WU's become one, and we have the CV "mora" needed earlier. This rule is considered to apply universally in level 1 phonology in the lexicon (see Kiparsky 1982; Mohanan 1981). It frequently reapplies at level 2 and post-lexically, though some languages do not require this reapplication. In this study I will assume the correctness of what has come to be known as "lexical phonology". While I do not assume that all languages necessarily have a lexicon recognizing levels (I would hope for a maximum of only two), it is assumed that all languages will have at least *some* phonological rules applying within the lexicon. The universal OCR is among these rules. Since it is coming to be accepted that the phonological rules applying in level 2 lexical phonology resemble those applying at what we might term "level 1 post-lexical phonology", the reapplication of the OCR at this level, or at these levels (if they are distinct), will be on a language-specific basis only.

The OCR accounts for two universal facts about [+cons] [-cons] sequences. First, it accounts for the fact that a [+cons] segment in this position will universally become an onset. There have been several proposals advanced to accomplish this, most recently Steriade's (1982) CV linking rule, which she also assumes to be universal. These other proposals, however, do not at the same time account for the second fact, which is that onsets do not contribute to phonological weight. The OCR crucially and necessarily relates these two facts: onset creation must take place in a [+cons] [-cons] transition and onsets do not have weight.

Let us see what the result of the OCR is for the Gokana tone mapping procedure which was discussed in relation to the verb form in (4). The underlying form of this verb is seen in (8a).

(8)   a.   H   (M)   L   b.   H   L   c.   H   L

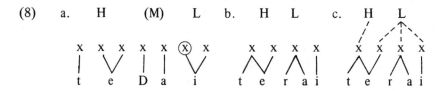

The morphemes involved are /teeD/ 'run' (with H tone), /-a/ (a meaningless "grade suffix" with no tone), /-ii/ '2nd person plural subject' (with M tone which deletes because of the upcoming L tone), and /ˋ/, a L tone conditioned by the zero tense when the subject is first or second person. (The circled first x of /-ii/ is deleted by a degemination rule discussed in Hyman (1982a, 1983) and in section 3.) In (8b) there have been two applications of the OCR: the x of both [+cons] segments of the verb root, i.e. /t/ and /D/, has been deleted because each x is followed by a [-cons] WU. (The phonological unit /D/ is an archiphoneme which in different phonological contexts is realized [l], [r] or [n]; see Hyman 1982b and section 7.) In both cases the consonants have reassociated to the x to their right. Finally, in (8c) we associate the H tone with the first x and the L tone with each of the remaining x's. As an automatic consequence of the OCR, we need not project only the vowels as TBU's, as would be required in the CV approach. We assign the tones to the x's, which then dominate one or more segments. Later it will be argued that the tone is automatically realized on the vowels, because the vowels are unspecified for tone, whereas the consonants are so specified in most cases.

We thus catch a glimpse of the relationship between this conception of the x-tier and the notion of a phonological projection: our x tier will in many cases preclude the necessity for projections.

In Gokana there is no evidence of syllable structure, as mentioned. In other languages, however, particularly languages which have consonant clusters, these x's provide the basis for syllable construction. The most common syllable types are seen in (9).

(9)

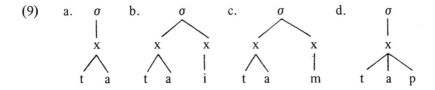

The universal CV syllable (with short vowel) has the representation in (9a), i.e. a syllable node dominating a single x with in turn dominates a CV set of features (where C = [+cons] and V = [-cons]). In (9b) and (9c) we observe that CVV and CVC syllables consist of a CV WU followed by a second WU having either a [-cons] or a [+cons] segmental matrix, respectively. (9b) and (9c) become the representations of heavy syllables in this approach: a heavy syllable is a syllable which branches! Or, equivalently, which has two (or more) x's. We do not need to refer to a rime projection, since everything we need will follow from the number of x's (minimum: 2) in determining a heavy syllable. Finally, in (9d), we allow for the possibility of a $CV^{[-son]}_{C}$ syllable to have a single WU. In Lithuanian, where vowels and sonorant consonants that are not onsets are potential tone-bearers, the syllable structures will exploit all four possibilities in (9): (9a) and (9d) will have only one TBU (x), and therefore will either have a H or L tone, while (9b) and (9c) will have two TBU's (x's) and will therefore have either HL or LH tone.

In order to derive the structure in (9d), we need only add a language-specific rule to affect the intermediate structure in (9c):

(10)

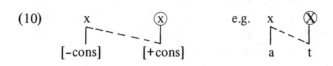

In Lithuanian this rule will further specify the [+cons] segment as necessarily [-son]. In other languages it will be possible either for there to be no such "margin creation rule" (MCR), in which case all postvocalic consonants remain weight-bearing, or for the MCR to affect all postvocalic consonants, in which case CVC syllables will always consist of a single WU (as in the syllable weight languages of type (b) in section 1). The MCR will thus have to be completely general in a language such as Huasteco, in which only CVV counts as a heavy syllable and CVC counts as a light syllable.

Additional rules will be needed to create complex onsets or margins in languages which allow consonant sequences within the same WU. These rules may of course obey a sonority hierarchy which, as demonstrated by Steriade (1982, 1983), may be partly universal, partly language-specific.

Chapter 3

Syllabicity without Syllables

In this section I would like to demonstrate that at least one language, Gokana, has syllabicity, but does not have syllables. Much of this section is based on Hyman (1982a, 1983a), although in these studies the x's on the x-tier stood for [+seg], while in the present study each x stands for a unit of phonological weight.

3.1. Defining syllabicity

Before considering the Gokana facts, it is necessary to establish what is meant by syllabicity. We are interested in this notion as it pertains to phonology, and indirectly in how it pertains to the phonetics of a [+syll] vs. [-syll] segment. There have been two basic approaches to phonological syllabicity: the feature approach and the syllable approach. A third approach, the weight approach, will be the one I adopt in this study. Let us consider each approach briefly.

(a) One of the clearest results of distinctive feature theory was to provide a meaningful way of distinguishing the major categories of segment types. While the Jakobsonian features [cons] and [voc] established the four categories "true" consonant ([+cons, -voc]), liquid ([+cons, +voc]), glide ([-cons, -voc]) and vowel ([-cons, +voc]), certain inadequacies of the system resulted in the rejection of the feature [voc] and the addition of the features [syll] and [son]. In the Chomsky and Halle (1968) feature system, the major categories are represented as in (11).

(11)	Obstr	V	G	N/L	N/L
[cons]	+	-	-	+	'+'
[syll]	-	+	-	-	+
[son]	-	+	+	+	+

Obstruents, nasals and liquids are [+cons], while vowels and glides are [-cons]. Obstruents are distinguished from the other categories by the feature [son], and differences in syllabicity are captured by the feature [syll]. Thus, syllabicity is represented directly in the feature system.[5] If we were to remove the feature [syll] from (11), we would not be able to distinguish (high) vowels from glides or syllabic from non–syllabic sonorant consonants. Something else would be needed.

(b) The other approach to syllabicity is to define it in terms of syllable structure: if a segment is in the nucleus of the syllable, it is syllabic; if it is in the onset or the margin of the syllable, it is not syllabic. In this approach, any [+syll] segment would have to therefore be assigned to the nucleus, e.g. a syllabic liquid or nasal. Whether an extrasyllabic consonant would be considered syllabic or non–syllabic is left unclear, since there seems to be some variation across languages (see below).

As pointed out in section 2, there is considerable redundancy in marking syllabicity in frameworks which have branching syllables: the syllable nodes confer a value of [syll], but the segments themselves may have the feature specified already. In a framework distinguishing C's and V's on the CV tier, there may even be a third redundancy.

The two assumptions I make in regard to syllabicity are as follows: (a) Each WU defines a "beat" or peak of sonority which can be referred to as "syllabicity". (b) This syllabicity is realized on the *most sonorous* segment dominated by each such WU. In other words, syllabicity in this framework is a consequence of *weight* and is defined independently of syllables. In addition, the location of each peak of syllabicity will depend upon the well–known sonority hierarchy which, among other things, places vowels above consonants, sonorants above obstruents, and so on. In this conception, an underlying representation such as in (12a)

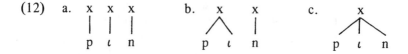

(12)   a.   x   x   x   b.   x   x   c.   x
           | | | ╱╲ | ╱│╲
           p   ι   n   p ι n   p   ι   n

treats the English word pin as having three "syllabic" units, since each segment is the most sonorous dominated by its respective WU. Each WU will represent a beat until or unless deleted. Thus, what the OCR says, in effect, is that a [+cons] segment may not have weight, i.e. syllabicity, if it is directly followed by a [–cons] segment, resulting in the representation in (12b). Here each of the two remaining WU's defines a syllabic beat. The peak of syllabicity will be realized on the [ι] of the first WU of (12b), not on the [p], which is lower than [ι] on the sonority scale. Note however, that a consonant which *follows* a vowel need not lose its weight, i.e. its syllabicity, by a (language–specific) MCR, since postvocalic syllabic consonants are well–formed in many languages. When a language such as Latin refers to the margin consonant as a "mora", i.e. as having weight, it in effect treats that consonant as syllabic. If on the surface the consonant in question is not syllabic, then an MCR must apply after the weight-sensitive rule in question (in this case, the Latin stress rule). In (12c) the MCR has applied to derive the English word [p^hɪn] with a single surface WU.

There is an important consequence and prediction made by this approach to syllabicity. This is that there cannot be an opposition between a syllabic x and a non-syllabic x. Consider the representations in (13).

(13)   a.

As seen in (13a), there can be no opposition between CV-C and CV-C, where in both cases the final C has an x of its own. This follows from my claim that a single feature matrix dominated by an x will be a syllabic segment. Now, whether this matrix remains syllabic throughout the phonological derivation will depend upon whether there is an MCR or other rule to remove its WU, in which case we obtain the representation in (13b). Thus, only consonants whose WU survives the entire derivation will be syllabic on the surface (assuming they are the most sonorous segment dominated by their respective WU). I assume that a language may contrast (13a) and (13b), i.e. that the same feature matrix may be syllabic in one case, but not in another (see section 4 for examples).

The CV tier, coupled with a branching syllable structure, makes the claim that the phonetic sequence in (13) may have the two different representations seen in (14).

(14)   a.   b.

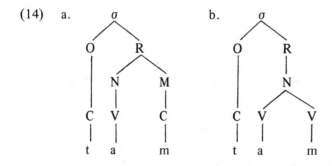

(14a) represents the final /m/ as being in the margin, i.e. as being [-syll], while (14b) represents it as being part of the nucleus and hence [+syll]. With projections being free to access either all elements of the rime, or only those dominated by the nucleus node (as per our two kinds of syllable weight languages in section 1), we can get two different possible oppositions: (a) In a language counting all elements of the rime, both

(14a) and (14b) would be heavy syllables, but they would be phonetically distinct, contrasting non-syllabic vs. syllabic [m] ; (b) In a language counting only elements of the nucleus, not only would the two be phonetically distinct, but also (14a) would be a light syllable, while (14b) is a heavy syllable. It is this second situation alone which is permitted by the WU analysis. What this means is that the theory of phonological weight is more restrictive than CV phonology in that it places stronger constraints on what a language may have or do vs. what it may not have or do. We will see many instances of this more constrained property of the theory developed in this study as compared to most other frameworks.

3.2. Gokana vowel length

In this section I shall present the basic properties of vowel length in Gokana and show how WU phonology is adequately equipped to deal with these properties. This section essentially summarizes the results reported in Hyman (1982a).

The basic segmental oppositions of the language are given in (15).

(15)	p	t	k^y	kp	(ʔ)		i		u		ii		uu
	b	d	g^y	gb			e		o		ee		oo
	f	s					ɛ		ɔ		ɛɛ		ɔɔ
	v	z						a				aa	
		l											
	[m	n	ɲ	ŋ]			ĩ		ũ		ĩĩ		ũũ
	/B̃	Ṽ D̃	Z̃	G̃/			ɛ̃		ɔ̃		ɛ̃ɛ̃		ɔ̃ɔ̃
								ã				ãã	

It will be observed that there are no glides in the language, though [v] and [z] derive historically from *w and *y, respectively, and that there are no underlying nasal consonants. As shown in Hyman (1982b), nasality is a prosodic feature on morphemes and is hence best represented as a feature [NASAL] on a separate autosegmental tier. A restatement of the nasal prosody is given in section 8 below, where the nasal consonants are represented as incompletely specified archisegments with certain of the consonant features spelled in according to whether there is a [+NASAL] autosegment associated with the archisegment (cf. the /D/ of (8a)). Finally, there are three tones in the language: [´] H(igh), [¯] (or unmarked) M(id), [`] L(ow). (The glottal stop in (15) is, in my analysis, inserted by rule; cf. section 4.1. below.).

The most remarkable fact about Gokana is that it allows vowel sequences of at least six units in length (identical and/or non-identical in nature). In (15) I have indicated a basic underlying contrast between single vowels and geminate vowels, which have respectively the structure in (16).

(16) a.   x   b.   x   x
            | \   /
                                        \ /
         [-cons]   [⁻cons]

Since there are no glides in Gokana, these representations are unambiguously syllabic. Two morphemes which have the geminate representation in (16b) are given in (17).

(17) a.   x   x   'him/her'   b.   x   x   'us, you pl.'
           \   /   \   /
            \ /   \ /
            E   i

In (17a) we see that the third person singular object clitic is represented as a geminate archisegment, i.e. as /EE/, whose vowel quality varies between [e] and [ɛ] according to whether the preceding vowel is [-low] or [+low], respectively. In (17b), the first/second person plural object clitic is a geminate /ii/. Both clitics become nasal if following a nasal morpheme.

What is important for the understanding of vowel length in Gokana is that these morphemes show an alternating vowel length, as seen in (18).

(18) a.   after C :   baè dìv-ee   baè dìv-ii   'they hit him /us'
      b.   after V :   baè sà-ɛ   baè sà-i   'they chose him/us'
      c.   after VV: baè sií-e   baè sií-i   'they caught him/us'

After a consonant, as in (18a), these clitics are realized with a geminate vowel, while after a vowel, whether single as in (18b) or geminate as in (18c), we observe that they are realized with a single vowel. A rule will be required to degeminate a geminate vowel which is preceded by a vowel. This rule will be formalized in a moment. First, let us observe the final verb form in (19).

(19)   mɛ́ɛ́ ɛ̀ kɔ m̄m̀ kɛ̀ɛ́-ɛ̀-ɛ̀-ɛ̀-ɛ́   'whoᵢ said I woke himᵢ up?'

These six identical vowel lengths of [ɛ̃] actually derive from eight *underlying* [-cons] WU's, as seen in the underlying representation in (20).

(20)   [+NAS]

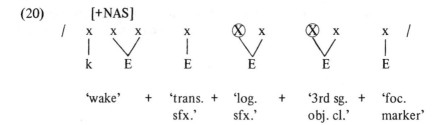

'wake'   +   'trans. + 'log. +   '3rd sg. + 'foc.
              sfx.'   sfx.'   obj. cl.'   marker'

The verb root has a geminate archisegment vowel /EE/ with a [+NAS] on the nasal tier. All of the suffixes have the same archisegment but without any feature on the nasal tier: the /E/ transitive suffix, the /EE/ logophoric suffix (see Hyman and Comrie 1981) responsible for the co-indexing of 'who$_i$' and 'him$_i$' in (19), the third person singular object clitic /EE/ and the focus marker /E/. In order to derive the six vowel lengths of (19) from the eight vowel lengths of (20), the degemination rule must apply *twice*. The WU's to be deleted in (20) have been circled.

Let us turn to the alternations seen in (21).

(21)   a.   tɔ   'house'   tɔɔ n ɛn   'house of person'
       b.   m ɛn   'neck'   m ɛ ǹ n ɛn   'neck of person'
       c.   mii   'blood'   mii n ɛn   'blood of person'

M tone nouns such as tɔ 'house', m ɛn 'neck' and mii 'blood' acquire a L tone "associative marker" when occuring as the head of a genitive construction. As seen in (21a), if the M tone noun ends in a short vowel, this vowel becomes long. The associative marker is thus represented as a WU with a L tone. The derivation of 'house of person' is given in (22).

(22)   M   L   M

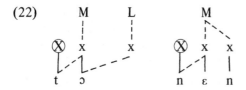

(I am ignoring the fact that the nasality in 'person' is from a separate nasal tier - see section 8.1) The underlying representation consists of the head noun /tɔ/ 'house' with two WU's and a M tone on the tonal tier, an associative marker consisting of a WU and a L tone on the tonal tier, and a possessor noun [nɛ̃n] 'person' (actually, /DĔD/) with three WU's and a M tone on the tonal tier. The processes indicated by the dotted lines and circled WU's take place as follows:

(i) The OCR deletes the first WU of each noun, associating their [+cons] onset consonant to the following WU.

(ii) Tone association takes place independently within each morpheme. The M of 'house' therefore associates with the one WU of that morpheme, the L of the associative morpheme with its one WU, and the M of 'person' to the *two* remaining WU's of 'person'.

(iii) The segmental matrix of the vowel /ɔ/ of 'house' adds a second association line to the right to acquire the WU of the L tone associative marker. This produces the desired double [ɔɔ̀] with the observed ML tonal contour.

The only rule that needs to be added to bring (22) to the surface is a very late one and concerns the final consonant of 'person'. As left in (22), the second [n] of 'person' is syllabic, since it has a WU, and it carries M tone. In reality it is non-syllabic and does not have its own tonal association. We therefore need a MCR which deletes the WU of a postvocalic consonant just in case it is associated to the same tone as the preceding vowel. This rule is formalized in (23).

(23)

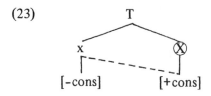

[-cons]   [+cons]

This rule both deletes the WU of the postvocalic consonant and reassociates its feature matrix to the preceding WU of the vowel. The reason for expressing this rule as such will be seen in our discussion of syllabic consonants in Gokana in section 4. Note that there is no danger of reassociating a sequence such as V.CV as VC.V, since the C in such a sequence will never be associated to the same tone as the preceding vowel. This results from the fact that the OCR has applied previously to remove its WU. Had there been any problem in excluding onset consonants from undergoing (23), it would be possible to indicate that the [+cons] WU in (23) must not branch.

Now that we have established that the associative marker consists of a L tone WU, why is it the case that the genitive constructions in (21b) and (21c) do not add an additional length to their head noun? That is, why don't we obtain *mɛnǹ nɛn and *miiì nɛn? As seen in (24), there is a need to delete a WU in cases where the head noun preceding the associative marker ends in either a geminate vowel or a consonant:

(24)   a.   b.

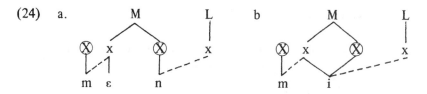

In both cases, the OCR removes the WU of the initial consonant, associating each onset [m] to the following x. In order to obtain the correct output seen in (21b,c), a rule must delete the circled x's in (24a,b). It turns out that this is exactly the rule needed to derive the single clitic forms in (18b,c). There, it is recalled, a geminate vowel degeminates when preceded by a vowel (whether geminate or single). This rule is formalized as in (25).

(25)   x $\otimes$ x   (degemination)

This rule says that whenever one has a geminate segment, i.e. two WU's joined together to a segmental matrix, as shown, which is preceded by a WU, the first x of the geminate is deleted. In order to prevent this rule from applying to forms having a consonantal onset preceding a geminate vowel, the first of the WU's of the geminate may not branch. (The reason why the second WU may also not branch will be seen in section 4.) This, then, accounts for the data in (18), as seen in (26).

(26)   a. $\otimes$ x $\otimes$ x x   b. $\otimes$ x $\otimes$ x   c. $\otimes$ x x $\otimes$ x

         d i v   e   s a ɛ   s i   e

The OCR removes the WU of the initial consonant in each case, as well as the WU of the [v] (underlyingly /B/) in (26a). This second application of the OCR thereby protects the first WU of the geminate clitic in (26a), since it branches and therefore cannot undergo (25). In the other two cases, the initial WU of the geminate clitic is preceded by an x and does not branch. Therefore it undergoes deletion by the rule in (25). Comparing the representations in (24), it is clear that the same rule will affect geminate vowels *and* geminate consonants. As will be seen in section 4, we are able to get a geminate consonant on the surface only in case the geminate consonant is itself followed by a vowel. When this latter circumstance obtains, the OCR has previously applied, making the second WU of the geminate branching and hence exempt from rule (25). In the case of the geminate consonant arising from the associative construction it is rarely the case that the L tone WU of the associative marker can be followed by a vowel, since all nouns (here the "possessor noun") begin with a consonant.[6]

3.3. No syllables in Gokana

In the preceding section we saw that WU's and syllabicity are intimately tied to one another, something which will become even clearer in our discussion of syllabic consonants in section 4. Particularly in the case of rule (25) we can observe that many of the rules that would have required feature specifications in other frameworks are expressable in geometric terms in WU phonology. We shall see other instances of this consequence of this theory in our discussion of epenthesis in section 5.

In this section I would like to claim that Gokana has no syllable structure, though as we have seen, it does have, as in the case of all languages, sylllabic and non-syllabic segments. It is of course logically impossible to prove that a language does not have syllables, since it may be the case that it has them but does not show obvious evidence of it - it may also be the case that some future linguist might discover evidence for the syllable in Gokana which I have simply overlooked. The argument will therefore have to be indirect, taking two forms. First, I shall continue the assertion made earlier that syllabicity can be captured without reference to syllables in Gokana, an argument which is continued in section 4.1. Since the WU's define syllabicity we do not need syllables in a language such as Gokana, which has no lexical consonant clusters.[7] Second, I shall attempt to show in the present discussion that the typical phonological properties which are sensitive to the syllable in other languages are sensitive to other units (the foot, the phonological word) in Gokana. Much of this section is taken from Hyman (1983a).

The arguments frequently advanced for syllable structure include the following: (i) Syllables may account for distributional constraints. (ii) Syllables may account for phonological processes (rules). (iii) Syllables may account for higher order units and processes. I shall argue that none of these arguments can be made for Gokana.

(a) *Distributional Constraints*. Frequently languages have different constraints of which consonants may be a syllable onset vs. which consonants may be a syllable margin. In particular, the class of syllable margins is usually more restricted than the class of syllable onsets. This may mean either the identity of the C which may occur in either position, or the nature of consonant clusters that may be permitted in one or the other part of the syllable, e.g. a language may allow a CC margin, but not a CC onset or vice-versa. Similarly, a language may restrict the class of vowels that can occur in a closed vs. open syllable, the former class being more limited than the latter. A case in point is Bamileke-Feʔfeʔ (Hyman 1972), where, for example, the only vowel that may appear before syllable-final /n/ is [ɛ] and the only vowel that may appear before syllable-final /d/ is [a].

Let us consider the distribution of consonants in Gokana. Lexical entries of nouns and verbs take the shape in (27).[8]

(27) C_i V (V) (C_j) (V)

In the case of nouns there is no internal structure. In the case of verbs, (27) may be divided into a root and a "grade suffix", e.g. $C_iV + C_jV$, $C_iVC_j + V$, etc. This is not relevant for possible evidence for the syllable for, as seen in (28), the non–initial C_j consonant may have only one of three values despite possible internal morphological structure:

(28)			*tautosyllabic*	*heterosyllabic*
a.	/B/ :	zob 'dance'	tóví 'throw'
b.	/D/ :	kil 'go'	zírá 'swear'
c.	/G/ :	pig 'mix'	tógí 'carve'

The three C_j consonants in question are the archiphonemes /B, D, G/, which have the realization [b, l, g] non–intervocalically and the realization [v, r, g] intervocalically. The restriction of the C_j consonant to one of these three phonological entities holds whether the C_j would be a syllable margin or a syllable onset in an analysis postulating syllables. The reason why I set up the incompletely specified archiphonemes /B, D, G/ is that these phonological units are realized as [m, n, ŋ] when there is a [+NAS] on the nasal tier, as seen in (29):

(29)			*tautosyllabic*	*heterosyllabic*
a.	/B/ :	dɛ̄m /dĒB/ 'mould'	dɔ́mí /dÕBi/ 'bite'
b.	/D/ :	bān /bāD/ 'beg'	tɛ́ní /tĒDi/ 'pass'
c.	/G/ :	ʔāŋ /āG/ 'yawn'	sɛ́ŋí /sĒGi/ 'economize'

(See section 8.1 for a discussion of nasality in Gokana and the archiphonemic representation of segments.) What the data in (28) and (29) indicate, then, is that the distribution of C_i vs. C_j consonants is effected without reference to position within a potential syllable. Instead of a distributional distinction between onset vs. coda, we have a distinction between initial vs. non–initial consonant, or between postvocalic vs. non-postvocalic consonant. This is the first hint that the syllable is irrelevant in Gokana phonology.

(b) *Phonological rules.* The second area where the syllable is frequently employed is in the statement of phonological processes or rules. Here too Gokana shows disregard for the syllable and instead a concern for "moras", i.e. our WU's. First, consider the fact that there may not be a L to M tonal contour within a foot.[9] The foot in Gokana is defined as a stem plus any lexical suffixes. These suffixes include derivational suffixes (e.g. causative, instrumental) and inflectional suffixes (e.g. second person plural subject, logophoric suffix). As seen in (30), the prohibition against a foot with a LM contour holds whether the tone bearing units, i.e. the vowels in this case, carrying the LM melody are tautosyllabic or heterosyllabic:

(30)   *tautosyllabic*   *heterosyllabic*
2nd pers. sg.:   oò dɔ̀ 'you fell'   oò bàn 'you begged'
2nd pers. pl.:   oò dɔi 'you fell'   oò banii 'you begged'
                         pl.   pl.
              /dɔ-ii/   /bãD-ii/
              L M   L   M

The L tone verbs /dɔ̀/ 'fall' and /bãD/ 'beg' are realized with their basic tone in the second person singular forms in (30). When the M tone suffix /ii/ '2nd pers. pl. subject' is added to these forms, however, the L of the verb stem must be deleted, because we would otherwise derive feet with LM contours. The LM contour would have been tautosyllabic in 'you pl. fell' (assuming that the ɔi sequence would belong to the same syllable), but heterosyllabic in 'you pl. begged'. Thus, the prohibition against LM sequences is foot-related, not syllable-related (cf. note 9).

Similarly, the harmonization of the mid front vowel takes place in Gokana without respect to syllable, as seen in (31).

(31)   *tautosyllabic*   *heterosyllabic*
a.   aè dɔ-ɛ̀ 'he$_i$ fell'   aè lɔr-ɛ̀ɛ̀ 'he$_i$ skinned'
b.   aè do-è 'he$_i$ measured'   aè zov-èè 'he$_i$ danced'

The logophoric suffix is represented underlying as /EE/ with L tone and signals that some referent is, roughly, coreferential with the person to whom an utterance is attributed in an indirect discourse (see Hyman and Comrie 1981). Its vowel length varies according to the rule in (25), as can be seen (cf. section 5.3., however). Its quality will be [+low], i.e. [ɛ] or [ɛɛ] when preceded by a [+low] vowel, as in (31a), but [-low], i.e. [e] or [ee] when preceded by a [-low] vowel, as in (31b). It will be [ɛ̃] or [ɛ̃ɛ̃] when nasalized, since the mid vowels [e] and [o] do not occur nasalized (cf. the vowel chart in (15) above). It can be noted in this regard that in addition to this vowel harmony process, nasalization spreads from left to right both within and across would-be syllable boundaries.

Finally, tone is assigned as a maximally bi-tonal melody within feet, with the first tone going on the first vowel and the second tone on any remaining vowels. An example was seen in (4), which we reanalyzed in terms of WU's in (8). The examples in (32) show that tone is a property of WU's in Gokana, not of syllables:

(32) a. kóò   (HL)   'friend'   (not *kô)
      b. dēè   (ML)   'hole'   (not *dḕ)
      c. dúū   (HM)   'dust'   (not *dē̄)

Except for a low-level juncture tone (see sections 4 and 8.2), two tones may not associate with a single vowel, as shown in the impossible forms given in parentheses.

(c) *Higher order units.* Turning to the possibility that Gokana may require syllables in the statement of higher order units or processes, we note first that foot structure is stated independently of syllables. The foot may not associate with a single vowel, as shown in the impossible forms by the formula in (33), in the case of verbs:

(33) Gokana foot structure: ROOT + GRADE + DER. + INFL.
                                       SFX   SFX.   SFX.

One could of course invoke a different term for this structure e.g. the "grammatical word", since it has a grammatical definition (it excludes, for example, the object clitics, which directly follow the inflectional suffix, if present), but it is the important unit in defining the distribution of C_j consonants, the prohibition of LM tonal contours, and the mapping of the bitonal melodies. On the other hand, vowel harmony and nasalization are properties of the phonological word, since these processes affect the object clitics and certain particles which immediately follow them, e.g. the focus and relativization particles.

It is perhaps significant that Gokana does not have any stress or accent to refer to syllables. And, finally, the reduplication process deriving gerundives from verbs does not refer to syllables, as seen in (34).

(34) a. CV verb   : dɔ   'fall'   →   dɔdɔ   'falling'
      b. CVC verb : dib   'hit'   →   didìb   'hitting'
      c. CVCV verb : darà   'pick up'   →   dadàrà   'picking up'
      d. CVVCV verb: piìgà 'try'   →   pipiìgà 'trying'

In this process the intial consonant and a single length unit of the initial vowel are copied. In the WU framework we would say that the first WU is reduplicated, not, of course, the first syllable.[10]

As was said earlier, the above arguments do not "prove" that Gokana does not have syllables. They do seem to indicate, however, that there is a conspiracy in the language to condition normally syllable-linked phenomena by other units (the foot, the "mora", etc.). If the above discussion does not fully justify this assertion, consider the difficulty of determining how to syllabify vowel sequences such as the form [kɛ̀ ɛ̀ ɛ̀ɛ̀ ɛ̄ɛ̄] seen earlier in (19). It was claimed that the six identical lengths of [ɛ̃] derive from eight underlying [-cons] WU's by two applications of the degemination rule in (25). The remaining six lengths will not be further subject to rule (25) because each of the suffixes now has a single [-cons] feature matrix, rather than the branching structure required for degemination. There seem to be three possible principles of syllabifying such sequences, though none of them is fully satisfactory. (i) We could assign a syllable node to each [-cons] WU. The verb form in (19) would thus have six syllables. We could assume a non-onset consonant to belong to the same syllable as the preceding vowel. In this proposal each mora is a syllable. Since the WU's have exactly the same segmental content as the would-be syllables, assuming that non-onset consonants have their own WU, the construction of such syllables would be at best redundant. (ii) We could assign a syllable node to each sequence of $CV^n(C)$, where V^n stands for however many vowels there are in sequence, and the parenthetical C is a non-onset consonant. This again provides a solution, but again, nothing follows from it. (iii) We could assign a syllable node to each sequence of (C) V (C, V), where the second consonant in parenthesis is a non-onset consonant. This would create syllables having either one or two WU's, i.e. CV, V, CV-C, V-C, CV-V and V-V. In this third proposal there would be a potention opposition between V-V (two WU's, one syllable) vs. V.V (two WU's, two syllables). As seen in (35a), we might further require that the definition of one vs. the other representation is that V-V contains only one [-cons] matrix, while V.V contains two.

(35) a.

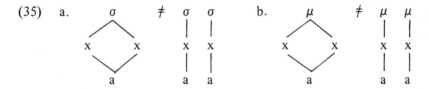

In this case there would be a redundancy between the number of syllables and the number of [-cons] feature matrices. However, as seen in (35b), there is also, at least in Gokana if not more generally, a redundancy between the number of [-cons] feature matrices and the number of morphemes. Thus, we don't even need syllables to refer to the number of matrices, since morpheme divisions, which are needed independently, will do the same job for us. Or, as François Dell put it, Gokana may be a language with heavy vs. light morphemes rather than heavy vs. light syllables. The representations in (35b) allow us to maintain a version of the obligatory contour principle (Leben 1973, 1978) whereby one may not have a sequence of two identical feature matrices within the same morpheme (cf. McCarthy 1981, who takes this position for the autoseg-mentalized consonant vs. vowel morphemes of Arabic).

One may arbitrarily choose one of the above alternatives, although there is no evidence to prefer one over the other. The lack of evidence for one or the other principle of syllabification thus lends further support to my claim that Gokana phonology is not structured on the basis of syllables. If it were, for one thing, it probably would not tolerate such long vowel sequences which may be ambiguous as to potential syllabification. The major advances made in the study of syllable structure have all come from languages with consonant clusters. Many of these studies do not address the question of multiple vowel sequences; for others it seems simply not to be interesting, since the assumption is made that each vowel will define a syllable. As just seen for Gokana, this is a simplistic view and is certainly wrong.

Chapter 4

Syllabic Consonants

In the preceding section I have attempted to demonstrate that while syllabicity may be universal, syllable structures are not. The universality of syllabic contrasts among segments, principally vowel vs. consonant, is attributable directly to the framework of WU's developed here: each WU is a beat and any beat which survives the entire phonological derivation will dominate a syllabic segment on the surface. Syllabicity will then be realized on the most sonorous segment dominated by the WU.

In order for this view to be completely convincing it must be demonstrated that differences in syllabicity among segment types can be adequately handled within WU phonology. In particular, we must be able to show that WU's are superior to C's and V's in capturing the properties of syllabic consonants. Such is the subject of this section.

Let us confine ourselves at first to the representation of syllabic sonorants – especially syllabic nasals, which are frequently present in languages, especially tone languages, where they are TBU's. Within the CV approach, the most obvious way to distinguish a syllabic nasal from a non-syllabic one is to have a V slot dominate the [+nasal] feature matrix.[11] There may seem to be some motivation for this in a language such as Dagur Mongolian which, it was reported in section 1, treats CVV and CVN as heavy syllables, but other CVC syllables as light (Austin 1952: 68).[12] If the nasal is dominated by a V slot, weight will be defined in CV phonology by a projection of the V units; or, if the nasal is assigned to the nucleus instead, by a projection of the slots dominated by the nucleus. Neither suggestion is completely explanatory, however. Martin (1961:19) transcribes this nasal as syllabic (his symbol is n̄, though I will write n̩). Let us assume for a moment that this segment consists of a [+cons, +nasal] feature matrix dominated by a V in the CV tier. Thus, any NC sequence will necessarily consist of a syllabic nasal, which follows from its representation as a V. Martin points out that "...whenever a vowel begins a particle the preceding n̩ → /n/ ...", i.e. the syllabic nasal loses its syllabicity in level 1 phonology. An example is seen in (36).

(36)   /saiŋ + ini/ → [sainini] 'as for the good'
        good – as for

In the CV approach the syllabic nasal + vowel transition is represented as in (37a).

(37)   a. V V   b. x x
            | | | |
            n i   n i

There is nothing in this representation that would predict that the syllabic nasal would become an onset onto the following vowel. Since the CV approach starts the syllabification off by linking a C and a V together (e.g. in Steriade 1982), a special rule would be required to change the V of the nasal in (37a) to a C. Or, the linking process would have to be restated as referring to the [+cons] [-cons] transition, in which case there is no need for C's and V's on the central tier.

In (37b), on the other hand, I have provided the representation for the same transition using a WU tier. It should be clear that this representation will automatically undergo the OCR to yield a single x dominating the two feature matrices. In other words, the desyllabification of the syllabic nasal in Dagur Mongolian (and other languages) follows without further stipulation from the concept of WU's developed in this framework.[13]

It is generally accepted that at the level of initial syllabification rules, a syllable may not consist of a syllabic consonant followed by a vowel. This follows automatically from the universal application of the OCR in level 1 phonology. In order for there to be a syllabic onset, it would have to have its own WU. However, the OCR guarantees that this will not be the case. Within many syllable-based frameworks (e.g. Steriade 1982), there is no explanation as to why a syllabic (or even non-syllabic) consonant + vowel sequence might not be assigned to the "rime", thereby obeying the principle that the onset must be non-syllabic. The generalization appears to be simply that a syllable may not begin with a syllabic consonant if it is followed by a vowel, *independently* of how this sequence might function within the syllable. Our approach, independent as it is from both the syllable and the rime, makes this correct prediction without further stipulation.

It is ironic that the WU approach, which does not overtly distinguish [+syll] and [-syll] as the CV approach does, seems better equipped to handle alternations between syllabic and non-syllabic consonants. In the following subsection we shall see that the same is true in Gokana, which has syllabic nasals. This subsection will be followed by discussions of potential counterexamples involving apparent cases of syllabic onset consonants, first from Kpelle, then from Idoma. In each case we will see that the WU framework provides a revealing account of the phenomena in question.

4.1. Syllabic nasals in Gokana

The discussion in this section supercedes that in Hyman (1983a). In Gokana there are three morphemes - pervasive ones - consisting solely of a syllabic nasal:

(a) The H tone syllabic nasal /Ń-/ is found among other places as a diminutive prefix on nouns (té 'tree', ń-té 'small tree', gà 'skewer', ŋ́ -gà ('needle') and occasionally on adjectives and independent pronouns (ńdígírí 'small', ńda 'mine').

(b) The first person singular morpheme, a bilabial nasal, seen in examples such as m̀ dáà 'I sleep', aè sà m̄ 'he chose me', and bá m̄ 'my arm' (=arm-me).

(c) The noun [ʔm̄ʔ] 'inside' and its verbal derivate 'to fill'.
In other words, we have either a homorganic nasal prefix of some sort, or a bilabial syllabic nasal morpheme. Let us consider the /Ń-/ prefix first.

It is not revealing to represent this prefix as a V on a CV tier, because its syllabicity is lost whenever its tone is identical to the tone of a preceding vowel, as seen in (38a).

(38)　a.　aè tú ŋ́ gà　[tú ŋ·gà?]　'he took a needle'
　　　b.　aè sà ŋ́ gà　　　　　'he chose a needle'
　　　c.　aè tú ágbá　　　　　'he took paint'

Since the nasal prefix in (38a) is preceded by a vowel having an identical H tone, the nasal loses its' syllabicity, as shown in brackets. In (38b), where the H tone nasal is preceded by a L tone, its syllabicity remains intact. (38c) shows that when the noun begins instead with a H tone *vowel* i.e. [-cons], this does not lose its syllabicity even if preceded by a vowel with the same H tone.

We already saw in (23) that when a single tone is associated onto a [-cons] [+cons] sequence, the WU is deleted. This is clearly what is needed in (38a). However, the representation of (38a) after application of the OCR given in (39) shows that there are *two* tones, albeit identical, associated onto the [-cons] [+cons] sequence:

(39)

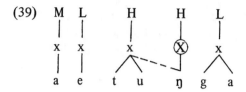

What we need to do then is to identify the /ú/ plus /ŋ́/ sequence, each with its own H tone as an input to the MCR in (23). This can be done either by reformulating this rule, though the result would be somewhat more complicated, or by invoking an equivalence condition akin to Leben's obligatory contour principle. Let us then assume that what is happening in (38a) is that rule (23) is removing the WU from the nasal consonant. The result is that [túŋ] has the same weight characteristics as a single morpheme such as [tům] 'pestle'. The only difference is in the nasality of the vowel in the latter form. In (38a) the vowel preceding the desyllabified nasal prefix is oral, since nasality may only spread from left to right (see section 8.1).

We have therefore derived desyllabification of syllabic nasals from the same process that "de-weights" postvocalic non-onset consonants. We can therefore avoid the changing from a V to a C on the CV tier which would be required in that framework. Consider now the phonetic pronunciations of the above nouns as they appear after pause:

(40)   a.   [ʔŋ̀gà ʔ] 'needle'   b.   [ʔágbá ʔ] 'paint'

The phonetic transcriptions in (40) represent how 'needle' and 'paint' are pronounced in isolation, i.e. with a pause boundary on each side. We shall not be concerned here with the final glottal stop, whose insertion before pause is conditioned by a number of irrelevant factors. The initial glottal stop (GS) is however easily inserted in the CV framework by the rule in (41).

(41) $\emptyset \rightarrow \underset{\underset{\text{ʔ}}{|}}{\text{C}}$ / [___ V

This rule inserts a GS, here a C unit with an associated GS feature matrix, whenever a V occurs immediately after a left bracket. The left bracket may be that of a stem, in which case a noun such as [ʔól] 'farm' has the underlying representation /óD/, or a phrase.[14] By treating the nasal prefix as an underlying V on the CV tier, GS insertion will automatically apply not only to vowel-initial nouns, but also to syllabic-nasal-initial nouns when appearing after pause, as in (40a).

In the x-tier approach, the GS insertion rule is expressed as in (42).

(42)   [x

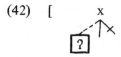

This rule states that a GS is inserted (insertion being indicated by a box around the GS) whenever the first WU following a left bracket does not branch. Given that the OCR precedes this rule, a glottal stop will not be inserted when a left bracket is followed by a branching WU, i.e. a [+cons] [-cons] sequence. It *will* apply to the syllabic nasal, however, since the latter's WU, like that of a true vowel, does not branch. Of course, rule (42) will have to apply before the MCR in (23), since the latter creates branching WU's of the [-cons] [+cons] type which are required nevertheless, as in the case of [ʔól] 'farm', to acquire an initial glottal stop. Thus, the possible advantage of the V representation of the syllabic nasal prefix – the ability to write GS insertion as in (41) – is not a real argument, since the geometrically conditioned rule in (42) is as straightforward and adequate. Note as a curious implication of rule (42) that the motivation behind this kind of frequent epenthesis is *not* that there be an onset node in every syllable, for Gokana does not have syllables. Instead, it is motivated by the requirement that a bracket–initial WU be branching. In particular, that it have a [+cons] left branch.[15]

Let us turn to the bilabial nasal morphemes. First, consider the alternation in length of the first person singular morpheme in the examples in (43).

(43)   a. bá-m̄ 'my arm'   b. bá-m̄-mí   'this my arm'

The syllabic nasal [m] 'my' in (43a) is the clitic form of this pronoun, identical in form to the object pronoun clitic. As a possessor it may be used only with body parts and other "inalienable" type nouns. It is normally syllabic, though it will lose its syllabicity if its tone is identical to that of the preceding vowel:

(44)   aè bunu bám niʔeí 'he broke my arm today' (from bá-m´)

The parenthetical floating H is observed before temporal and locative expressions (see Hyman 1983a and below), here before the temporal adverb niʔeí 'today'. It is assigned to the clitic, turning it into a H tone, thereby making the nasal identical in tone to the H of bá 'arm'. As in the case

of the H tone nasal prefix, the intermediate form bá-m̀ must undergo
the MCR in (23) to yield [bám].

Turning to (43b), we note that when the bilabial syllabic nasal is
followed by a vowel, it is realized as a geminate whose second WU undergoes the OCR to create an onset for the following vowel. The vowel in
question in (43b) is the demonstrative /í/, cf. bá-í 'this arm'. How is the
gemination to be explained? We can propose, as I did in Hyman (1983a),
that the extra length unit (whether a C or an x) is inserted. There is, however, good reason to believe that it instead is part of the underlying form
of the clitic. We saw in (18) that the third person singular and first/second
person plural object pronouns alternate between geminate and single.
The gemination rule in (25) was proposed to account for this alternation.
Since these other clitics have an underlying geminate representation, I
propose to represent 'me, my' as in (45a).

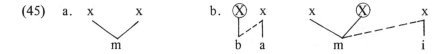

(45)   a.   x   x   b. Ⓧ x   x   Ⓧ   x
              \   /   ⌐ ⌐1   \   /   ⌐ ⌐ ⌐ ⌐ ⌐1
                m   b   a   m   i

The representation for 'this my arm' ('this arm of mine') is given in (45b).
As seen, the exact required output [bám̄mí] is obtained by two applications of the OCR! The first application removes the x of the /b/; the
second removes the second x of the geminate nasal. In both cases the
[+cons] segment associates to the following [-cons] WU, as per the
OCR. Thus, by representing 'me, my' as in (45a), we can capture the
length facts in a natural way, requiring no rules other than the ones we
have set up for other purposes. Finally, we now can note in the output
of (45b) why it was necessary to formalize the degemination rule as it
was presented in (25). The degemination rule (DGR) has to specify that
the *second* WU of a geminate does not branch or else it will apply to the
output of (45b), incorrecting yielding *bám̄í. The need for requiring that
the first WU of the geminate not branch has already been explained.

How would the alternation in (43) be captured in CV phonology? First,
someone might try to claim that the onset creation observed when a so-
called syllabic nasal is immediately followed by a vowel is universal, and
should be accomplishable automatically. Mohanan (1979), for instance,
suggests that syllabic consonants are universally ruled out between vowels,
i.e. one cannot have V-Ṇ-V. This is undoubtedly true in level 1 phonology, though the following Igbo example shows that such sequences
are possible in later derived environments:

(46)   úlọ̀ m̀ ò tèrè ányá 'is my house far?'

In this example the syllabic nasal /ḿ/ 'my' carries a H tone flanked by a L tone on each side. There is no question as to its syllabicity (though there might have been if the preceding vowel carried the same tone). Since Mohanan's observation holds only in level 1 phonology, the post-lexical intervocalic syllabic nasal in (46) is allowed to surface in Igbo. In any case, something language specific is required to explain why the syllabic nasal becomes a geminate before a vowel in Gokana, but only degeminates in Dagur Mongolian, as seen above in (36).

A reasonable argument that might be made from a CV framework is that the nasal morpheme in question has a VC structure. This would automatically provide the C that is needed for the onset in (43b), but it would not explain why the morpheme, now analyzed as $\underset{m}{\overset{V}{\smile}}C$, would degeminate in (43a). Since the remaining single unit of length is "syllabic", we would have to propose that it is the C which is deleted in bá m̄. However, the tonal facts argue that it is the *first* unit, here the sole V, which must be deleted. Consider first the tones found with the third person singular clitic in (47).

(47) a. mɛ̃n-ɛ́ɛ̃   'his/her neck'   mɛ̃n-ím̄   'my neck'
      b. bǔ-ɛ̃   'his/her pus'   bǔ-m̄   'my pus'
      c. mií-ɛ̃   'his/her blood'   mií-m̄   'my blood'

In each example the noun carries an underlying M tone. In (47a), where the clitic follows a consonant and therefore does not undergo the DGR, there is no tonal change: the underlying HM melody of the clitic is realized on the clitic itself. In (47b) and (47c), on the other hand, where the clitic is preceded by a M tone vowel and must undergo the DGR, we observe that the H of the HM clitic is assigned onto the preceding WU. The result is a MH contour in (47c) but a single H tone in (47b), since the language generally forbids associating two tones to a single WU.

Now let us turn to the corresponding first person singular clitic forms in (47) and (48), the latter containing the equivalent object clitic (cf. (18) for the third person singular object clitic):

(48) a. aè dìv-im   'he hit me'
      b. aè sà-m̄   'he chose me'
      c. aè sií-m̄   'he caught me'

When preceded by a consonant in (48a), the nasal clitic acquires an epenthetic [i] (see below). Otherwise, like the third person singular clitic in (47b,c), it degeminates and sends its H tone onto the preceding vowel in (48c). Thus, if in the CV analysis we were to delete the C, we would not only lose the parallelism with the VV clitics, but we would also have complications in predicting the tones in (48b,c). Of course, if we represented the nasal clitic as a VV we would require a special rule to change the second V to a C when the geminate nasal is followed by a vowel. While a V to C rule would work in establishing the needed onset in (43b), as well as in (36) in Dagur Mongolian, the advantage of the WU approach is that the OCR automatically accomplishes this same onset creation without resort to a special ad hoc rule for syllabic nasals.

Since the epenthetic [i] came up in the form in (48a), a word must be added concerning it. It would be tempting to set up the first person singular clitic as /im/. However, there is a problem with this. First of all, the [i] in (48a) is [-nasal]. Since nasality is a morphological feature and is represented as a [+NAS] specification on the nasal tier (see section 8.1), the only representation we have for [im] is / ĩB/. The [+NAS], indicated by the raised tilde, should then be associated onto both the vowel and the archisegment to yield *[ĩm]. To prevent this from happening, I propose the following vowel epenthesis rule:

(49)

$$\begin{array}{ccc} \text{x} & & \text{x} \\ \text{[+cons]} & \boxed{\text{i}} & \text{[+cons]} \end{array}$$

Within the lexical phonology, if a [+cons] WU is followed by a [+cons] WU which doesn't branch, the epenthetic vowel [i] is inserted. This insertion thus adds the epenthetic vowel to the x preceding the nasal morpheme, hence the [+NAS] of the latter will not affect it. Since [+NAS] associates only from left to right, the epenthetic vowel will only be nasalized if *preceded* by a [+NAS] morpheme, as in [mɛn- ím̄] 'my neck'.

A second argument is perhaps even stronger. In (50) we observe both the epenthetic vowel *and* a geminate nasal:

(50)

$$\begin{array}{ccccccc} \text{Ⓧ} & \text{x} & \text{x} & & \text{x} & \text{Ⓧ} & \text{x} \\ \text{m} & \text{ɛ} & \text{n} & \text{i} & \text{m} & & \text{i} \end{array}$$ [mɛním̄mí] 'this my neck'

As seen in the underlying representation, the nasal clitic is underlyingly a geminate and the [í] is inserted. The reason why the nasal is not geminate in (48a), then, is because the DGR in (25) has applied to delete the geminate's first WU. The epenthesis of the [i] is not really needed to trigger the DGR, since the x of the preceding consonant would have satisfied the left environment. However, in (50), the DGR cannot apply because the second WU of the geminate nasal branches. Thus, degemination has to do with the DGR in (25), while epenthesis has to do with the unacceptability of two [+cons] matrices in sequence, where the WU of the second is not an onset (i.e. does not branch, as indicated in the formulation of this rule in (49)).

The VC analysis is to be dispreferred for another reason, which requires that we consider the third source of syllabic nasals in Gokana: the noun 'inside'. This word is pronounced [ʔm̄ʔ] in isolation. The initial GS is inserted by rule (42); the final GS is present only before pause and is also inserted by rule. The noun has an underlying M tone. As seen in the forms in (51), this noun requires the same representation as the clitic 'me, my':

(51) a. [ʔm̄-mí] 'inside this'   b. [ʔm̄-má̆ʔ] 'inside that'

In (51) the demonstratives /í/ 'this' and /á/ 'that' (the latter acquiring a GS before pause), when added to the noun 'inside', provide for the same gemination observed in (43b), Thus, if 'me, my' has a VC structure, so does the noun 'inside'.

Now to' the problem. This same noun has verb derivatives formed with the intransitive suffix /-a/ and the transitive suffix /-È/, as seen in (52).

(52) a. [ʔm̄-má̆]   'to fill' (intr.)   (cf. bír-á 'become black')
      b. [ʔm̄-mɛ̆ʔ] 'to fill' (tr.)   (cf. bír-è 'blacken (sth.)')

Again, since these suffixes are [-cons], a geminate nasal is required. This would follow either from the xx analysis of the root 'inside' or from the VC analysis. However, a choice is possible when we consider the realization of verb forms with the -ma 'with' suffix.

Representative derivations involving the 'with' suffix are provided in the examples in (53).

(53) a. /kpɔ́/ [kpɔ́ʔ]   'cut'   → [kpɔ́ɔ́-má̆] 'cut with'
      b. /buD/ [bul]   'cook'   → [bu-má̆]   'cook with'
      c. /da - Dà/ [darà]   'pick up' → [daà-má̆]   'pick up with'
      d. /ZáD - í/ [záríʔ]   'buy'   → [zá-má̆]   'buy with'

In (53a) we see that -ma adds an extra vowel length to a preceding CV verb stem. In (53b) we see, on the other hand, that the final consonant of a CVC verb stem falls before the -ma suffix. (Note that (49) does not insert epenthetic [i] because the following [+cons] WU branches.) Now, concerning verbs that already have a suffix (a "grade suffix" in the two examples), we see in (53c) that -ma replaces a -CV grade suffix, and the preceding vowel lengthens as in (53a). Similarly, in (53d), -ma replaces a -V grade suffix, and the preceding consonant drops as in (53b). The question now is, what about the forms in (52) with a syllabic nasal? If the underlying representation of the forms in (52) is VC-V, we should expect this to become VC-ma, and then for the C to drop, as in (53b,d), yielding [ʔm̩-ma᷄]. As seen in (54), however, this is not what is found:

(54)   /m̩m + a/ , /m̩m + È/ → [ʔm̩-m̩-ma᷄] 'fill with' (intr/tr)

The intransitive/transitive distinction is lost in the 'with' from. As seen, there are three [m] lengths separated by hyphens: two syllabic lengths (or WU's) and one non-syllabic (onset) length. This cannot be gotten directly from the VC representation, but rather would result from representing the root as a single V with an associated /m/. In this case we would derive the correct output in (54), but we would not be able to account for the additional length unit acquired as an onset when followed by a vowel (verb suffix or demonstrative etc.).

Let us now look at the derivation of the above forms within the WU framework. Assuming a double x analysis of the morpheme 'inside', we have the following derivations for the verbs in (52).

(55)   a.   x   Ⓧ   x   (intr.)   b.   x   Ⓧ   x   (tr.)
                  m   a   m   ε

As we have seen in many examples, a single application of the OCR creates the right outputs (with GS insertion (42) applying, as well as prepausal GS being inserted after the transitive suffix as seen in (52b)). As for the 'with' forms, I assume that there is an additional "floating" x unit preceding the segments of the suffix. The derivation of (53a,b) would therefore take place as in (56).

(56)   a.   Ⓧ   x   x   Ⓧ   x   b.   Ⓧ   x   Ⓧ   x   Ⓧ   x
                  kp   ɔ   m   a   f   u   l   m   a

As seen, there are two applications of the OCR in each case. The floating x preceding the -ma suffix acquires an association from the preceding segment: in (56a) the vowel /ɔ/, in (56b) the consonant [l] (from /D/). The single [l] associated to two x's will undergo the DGR (25), deleting the first of the two x's, as indicated. The remaining rule that is needed is the one deleting the [+cons] WU and its feature matrix preceding the -ma suffix, seen in (57).

(57)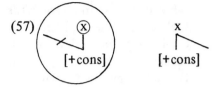

What this rule says is that the WU and [+cons] segment are deleted if (a) the [+cons] is not also associated to the preceding WU (in which case we would have the geminate [ḿ̄ṁ] observed in (54)); and (b) it is followed by a [+cons] WU which branches. This second condition blocks [i] epenthesis in (56b), though it may be superfluous since the epenthesis rule applies post-lexically only after the syntactic process of pronoun cliticization has taken place.

Now let us turn to the derivation of (54):

(58)

The [m] of the root 'inside', already associated to two WU's associates to a third one in (58): the floating x of the 'with' suffix. This yields *three* syllabic lengths, i.e. *ḿ̄ṁṁá. At this point the DGR deletes the second WU of the triple nasal. The OCR is, of course, responsible for the deletion of the WU of the [m] of the 'with' suffix.

As a last illustration of the above rules, consider the derivation of [m̄-mí-m̄] 'inside me':

(59)   a.   [lexical]

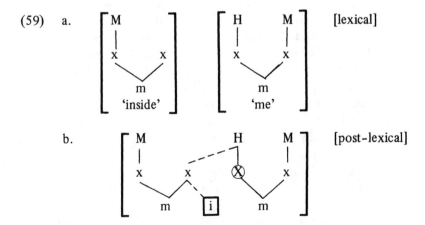

       b.   [post-lexical]

We begin with the two lexical entries 'inside' and 'me', both consisting of two WU's having joint custody of a single segmental matrix /m/. The first morpheme has only a single M tone, which associates onto the first WU, while the second morpheme associates its HM melody onto its two WU's, as shown in (59a). When cliticization takes place post-lexically in (59b), the phonological derivation requires the following three rules: (a) [i]-epenthesis (49); (b) the DGR (25), removing the first WU of the morpheme 'me'; and (c) association of the H freed up by the deletion of its WU onto the available WU to its left.

4.2. Syllabic onsets in Kpelle

Having demonstrated that the WU framework provides a more explanatory account of weight phenomena and its relation to syllabicity, particularly in the case of syllabic consonants, we now turn to a case in the literature where it has been claimed that a language, Kpelle, has syllabic [+cons] onsets. Since the OCR is designed to remove the WU of a [+cons] segment which becomes an onset, the question arises as to how or whether this can be possible in languages.

First described by Welmers (1962), Kpelle, a Mande language spoken in Liberia, shows a number of initial consonant mutations involving voicing and nasality. The following table gives examples of the relevant alternations:

(60)	Stem	'my'	'his/her' (Welmers)	'his/her' (Dwyer)	
a.	pólù	m̀bólù	bólù	bbólù	'back'
	túɛ́	ńdúɛ́	dúɛ́	ddúɛ́	'front'
	kɔ́ɔ́	ŋ̀gɔ́ɔ́	g̀ɔ́ɔ́	g̀gɔ́ɔ́	'foot, leg'
	kpíŋ	ŋ̀gbíŋ	g̀bíŋ	g̀gbíŋ	'self'
	fíí	m̀víí	v̀íí	v̀víí	'hard breathing'
	súá̂	ńzúá̂	z̀úá̂	z̀zúá̂	'nose'
b.	ɓāráŋ	m̄āráŋ		m̄āráŋ	'companion
	lēē	ńēē		n̄ēē	'mother'
	wólí	ŋʷólí		ŋʷólí	'ear'
	yéé	ɲéé		ɲéé	'hand, arm'
c.	mālóŋ	m̄ālóŋ		m̄ālóŋ	'misery'
	náŋ	ńáŋ		ǹáŋ	'father'
	ŋɛ́ì	ŋ́ɛ́ì		ǹɛ́ìŋ	'eye
	ŋʷāŋ	ŋ̄ʷāŋ		ŋ̄ʷāŋ	'double arm span'
	ɲíŋ	ɲíŋ		ɲíŋ	'tooth'

As seen, the stem consonants group into three series: (a) voiceless obstruents; (b) oral sonorants (assuming that the bilabial implosive is a sonorant (cf. Kaye 1982), who claims that implosives should be analyzed as liquids); and (c) nasal sonorants. The stem–initial consonants are presented in their underlying forms, which is how they appear, for instance, after the possessive pronoun í 'your', e.g. í pólù 'your back'. All of the nouns in (60) belong to the "relational class", essentially the so-called nouns of inalienable possesion. The possessive pronouns are different for non-relational nouns (see Welmers 1969).

In column 2 we see that after the possessive pronoun /Ń/ 'my', the voiceless obstruents of group (a) become voiced and the initial sonorant consonants of groups (b) and (c) drop. The nasal-oral opposition on stem-initial sonorants is, however, preserved, since the vowel(s) following a stem-initial nasal consonant will have become nasalized prior to the dele-tion of the consonant. Thus, from /Ń + lée/ we obtain [ńéé] 'my hand' (with oral vowels), while from /Ń + γɛ́í/ (with a [+NAS] on the nasal tier) we obtain [ŋɛ̃́í] 'my eye'. As seen in the latter representation, nasality is considered to be an autosegmental feature on morphemes, much as in Gokana, here not only nasalizing the two vowels in 'eye', but also creating a velar nasal consonant from an underlying gamma.

The issue that immediately arises as one considers the (b) and (c) forms for 'my' + NOUN' is that the onset has a tone, which would seem to require that the onset have a WU of its own. Presumably the 'my' forms are distinct phonetically from the zero or stem forms in the case of group (c). Thus, a H toned onset nasal consonant is not equivalent to an untoned onset nasal consonant, even if the latter is followed immedi-ately by a H tone vowel.

The forms in (60) and others like them generated a heated debate over a period of ten years or so, starting with responses to Welmers' analysis including Manessy (1964), Meeussen (1965), Bird (1971), Hyman (1973a) and Dwyer (1974). Welmers' transcriptions of the 'my' forms is accepted by Manessy and Dwyer, who have intimate knowledge of the South-western Mande languages, though Bird, also a specialist in these languages, provides transcriptions such as ḿmáráŋ 'my companion', i.e. with a syl-labic nasal followed by a non-syllabic nasal onset. In the 'his/her' forms, Dwyer provides a different transcription from that of Welmers, at least as concerns the nouns in group (a). Welmers actually "phonemicizes" forms such as 'his/her back' as /`pólù/, i.e. with a floating L tone which is the mark of the 'his/her' morpheme. He states that this tone has the effect of creating heavily voiced obstruents and lowering the pitch on the following vowel. In the case of the nouns in group (b), it actually is realized as a nasal, something which cannot readily be derived from a floating L, as the critics of Welmers' analysis have pointed out. The proper derivation involves an underlying /Ǹ/ for 'his/her' and a rule (a) voicing obstruents and (b) nasalizing sonorants after a homorganic nasal. In the last column of (60) it is seen that Dwyer reinterprets Welmers' heavy voiced obstruents with L tone as geminates. He proposes that the NN sequences resulting

from the post–nasal assimilation rule be degeminated by a nasal simplification rule: "Nasal Simplification reduces a sequence of two identical
nasals to a single nasal segment. Without this rule, surface geminate nasals,
for which there is no acoustical evidence, would be derived" (p. 67).

Assuming the above account, the single rule voicing the obstruents
/p, t, k, kp, f, s/ to [b, d, g, gb, v, z] and nasalizing the oral sonorants
/b, l, γ, w, y/ to [m, n,ɲ , ŋ, ŋ ʷ] after the two homorganic nasal morphemes is formalized in (61a), and the rule creating geminate consonants
is formalized in (61b).

(61)   a.   b.

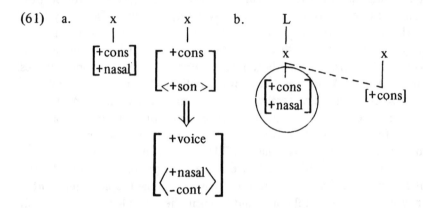

(I ignore for our purposes the fact that nasality is on a separate tier.) It
should be noted with respect to (61a) that I am considering glides in
Kpelle to be [+cons] (see section 6 below). Thus, the only changes that
need to be made in the nasalization process are [+nasal] and [–cont]
(and perhaps also [–lat], if relevant). In (61b), a nasal consonant matrix is
deleted, and the following [+cons] matrix (now either a voiced obstruent
or a nasal stop by (61a)) associates to its WU. (61b) crucially refers to the
L tone of 'his/her', while the nasal in (61a) may be either of a H or L
tone morpheme.

The derivation of [b̀bólú] 'his/her back' thus proceeds as in (62).

(62)   (a)   (b)   (c)

In (62a) the two underlying morphemes have been separated by a left
bracket indicating that pólù is a stem. As seen in (62a), the OCR has
two applications, creating two branching WU's. In (62b) homorganic

nasal assimilation applies and the tones have been assigned on a one-to-one basis to the three surviving WU's. Also, the shorter expansion of (61a) has voiced /p/ to [b]. The final step in the derivation occurs in (62c), where rule (61b) has deleted the nasal consonant matrix and associated the following [b] to its WU. The result is the desired geminate [bb].

A similar derivation is needed with respect to [ǹēē] 'his/her mother', which deriving from /Ǹ + lēē/ runs the risk of violating the OCR:

(63)

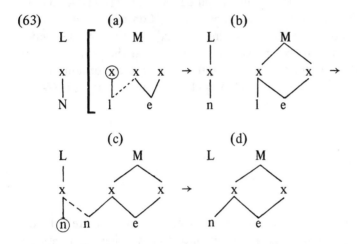

In (63a) the OCR removes the WU of the stem-initial /l/. In (63b) homorganic nasal assimilation and tone association take place. In (63c) the longer expansion of (61a) converts /l/ to [n] and (61b) creates a single geminate. At this point we have derived [ǹnēē]. However, as the passage cited from Dwyer (1974) above indicates, the surface nasal is not geminate. In order to degeminate it, it is clear that it must be the *first* of its x's which is deleted, yielding the output in (63d). At this point we can choose to reassociate the L to the first of the two remaining WU's, in which case this WU will have a LM transition in it. Or perhaps one could leave the L unassociated with its effect being felt "syntagmatically". In other words, just as Clements and Ford (1979) have proposed treating tonal downstep as an unassociated L causing the following (associated) H tone to be interpreted at a lower pitch than a preceding H, this free L tone could serve as an input to the phonetic interpretation rules which would introduce the lowering and the heavy voicing as "detail rules".

This second alternative, which may not seem to have as much merit as the first when the initial, affected consonant is a sonorant, may be more attractive when this consonant is an obstruent. Recall that there is some disagreement as to whether the initial consonant in forms such as 'his/her back' is geminate (as claimed by Dwyer) or single (as assumed by everyone else). Consider what Dwyer has to say about this: "Voiced geminate consonants in Kpelle have been described by Welmers (1962) as having 'heavy voicing'. Heavy voicing means that the period of duration of voicing is longer than that used for a normally voiced obstruent. The use of a geminate consonant adequately expresses this fact. Furthermore, the use of geminate consonants permits a fairly natural derivation of surface consonants with extra heavy voicing" (p. 70). While Dwyer's observation about the pronunciation of these obstruents is consistent with his analysis, the setting up of geminates is not required. Bird (1971) in fact had invoked Maran's (1971) glottal features Spread, Constricted, Raised and Lowered to capture the "heavy voicing" vs. "regular voicing" distinction that Kpelle appears to require. Given, therefore, that the geminate representation in (62c) is not absolutely required, we have the option of deleing the initial WU exactly as we did in (63d), yielding the output in (64).

(64)

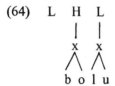

With (64) we are now much closer to Welmers' floating L representation, and the same question arises as before concerning whether the floating L should reassociate to the WU to its right. If not, then its interpretation by the phonetic detail rules will be (a) to cause "heavy voicing" (perhaps slightly lengthening the duration of the obstruent), and (b) to cause slight lowering of the H tone assigned to the first x.

If the L is allowed to associate onto the initial WU of (63d) and (64) we will appear to have a LM rising tone. The question thus arises as to whether any language can contrast a hypothetical [ČV] vs. [CV̌], i.e. where in the one case the transition of tonal contour takes place in going from the onset consonant to the vowel, while in the other case the complete contour is realized on the vowel (=the normal case, where contour tones are found in tone languages). In all likelihood the first representation is equivalent to the "depressor consonants" found in Southern Bantu languages, which McLaughren (1984) has recently analyzed as having an opaquely associated L tone. If the L in the Kpelle forms associates to the word-initial WU one will have the impression, at least, of a "syllabic" onset, whether a sonorant or an obstruent. Now the OCR does not in itself forbid such a representation. It merely forbids a [+cons] WU from appearing before a [-cons] WU within the lexical phonology. The problem of having to *block* the OCR so that the nasal of [n̈e͞e] does not lose its WU does not arise in the derivation in (63), because of our formulation of consonant deletion in (61b). An alternative analysis which would have raised the possibility of blocking the OCR would have been to conceive /Ǹ + lēē/ as becoming [ňēē] through deletion of the /l/, as in (65a).

(65) a. L   M   b. L   M

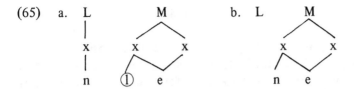

This would leave an [n] with a L tone x followed by an [e] with a M tone x. Hence the OCR should apply. However, if syllabicity means having a WU, and if the onset in [ňēē] is syllabic, then, it might be claimed, the OCR should be blocked. But if it is blocked, e.g. in the case where there is a tone preassociated on the [+cons] WU, then it can't be universal. As seen in the above analysis and the derivation in (63), we provide for representations such as (65b), whether or not the floating tone reassociates to the first WU.

It can be concluded, then, that there is no way to block the OCR within the (level 1) lexical phonology. Only if the lexical phonology does not reapply at level 2, or only if the relevant environment is created postlexically, may the OCR be prevented from applying, as perhaps in the case of the syllabic nasal in the Igbo sentence given above in (46). Thus, where the OCR appears to be violated on the surface, since there is a syllabic [+cons] segment followed by a [-cons] segment, we either are dealing with a major syntactic boundary or with a complex derivation such as the one just seen in Kpelle.

4.3. Syllabic liquids in Idoma

The Idoma language described by Abraham (1951/1967), a Kwa language spoken in Nigeria, shows consonant + liquid + vowel sequences where the liquid, usually /l/, appears to be tone-bearing:

(66) a. pĺ-à   'deceived'   c. à-gĺ-ágbà   'trousers'
      b. ú-dŕ-ō   'navel'   d. kpĺ-á   'borrowed'

These forms are given with the hyphens established by Abraham to indicate the syllabicity of the postconsonantal liquids, about which he states: "A consonant follwed by 'l' or 'r'... employs these two sounds as vowels, not as consonants, the combination forming one syllable..." (p. 13). There is clearly only one underlying liquid in Idoma, /l/, which after certain consonants varies with [r]. The Idoma consonant system is given in (67), as I have been able to ascertain it from Abraham's work:

(67) p   t   č̌   k   kp
      b   d   j   g   gb
      f   h
              l   y   w
      m   n   ɲ   (ŋ)   ŋm

All of the above consonants may appear in the onset position before a vowel except /ŋ/, whose distribution is limited mostly to post-vocalic (i.e. syllable final) position and to its realization in syllabic form, especially when preceding a velar consonant, as in èɲ̀ŋ̀kp̄ɔ̄ 'water', It therefore automatically would not appear before syllabic /l/. The remaining consonants not found before syllabic /l/ are the palatals /č j y ɲ /, the labiovelar glide /w/, and the alveolar sonorant consonants /l/ and /n/. The last two may not appear in this position because of their phonetic similarity with /l/. Perhaps the glides /y/ and /w/ would not be followed by a syllabic sonorant consonant for the same reason, although /y/ is out also for the same reason that the other palatal consonants are out. This reason appears to be that instead of getting a palatal consonant + /l/ + vowel, we obtain palatal consonant + i + /l/ + vowel, e.g. čílá, jílà, etc. Whether this [i] is underlying or epenthetic will not be addressed here.

The question is: how can the framework developed in the previous sections permit a CL̩V "syllable" (assuming that this does constitute a single syllable)? Our OCR would provide the derivation in (68):

(68)   a.   H   L   b.   H   L

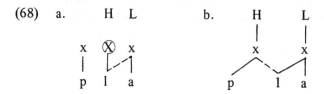

The WU of the /l/ is deleted by the OCR as it becomes the onset on the following WU, as seen in (68a). This might seem counterintuitive, since it is supposed to be the liquid that is a "vowel", according to Abraham. In fact, in CV tier analysis, we might represent such "syllables" as CVV, in which case there would be no problem, since no change would be needed to get the H on the liquid and the L on the vowel. That this is not right is seen from the following observation made by Abraham: "This 'l' never occurs after 'm', but when we have 'ml', it is the 'm' which is syllabic...." (p. 108). He gives the examples m̀-lɛ̀ 'swallowed' and m̀-lùwā 'with them'. Now the representation in (68a), if followed by tone association, would produce just this result in the case of /ml/ sequences, whereas the CV account would have to have some kind of rule changing the CVV to a VCV representation, presumably. What about syllabic /l/, then? As seen in (68b), tone association puts the first tone on the first WU (here the consonant /p/) and the second tone on the second WU. Because the /p/ is not sonorous enough to carry the tone, an additional association line is drawn from the /l/ to the first WU, as shown in (68b). The result is a "syllabic" [l], which is actually equivalent to a geminate. The fact that this sequence derives from an earlier CVLV sequence helps to explain the special processes involved here (cf. Trutenau's 1972 discussion of a similar situation in Gã).

The peculiar behavior of nasal + liquid sequences is thus explained and is predicted from the fact that Idoma has the OCR, as do all languages, and does not permit WU's with the structure CCV, i.e. with a consonant sequence as the onset to a WU. I suspect that as we apply the WU framework to other languages with "peculiar" syllabicity problems, more such phenomena will fall into place and cease to elude us.

4.4. Syllabicity and extra-syllabicity

In all of the preceding examples we have seen that syllabicity depends on having an x on the weight tier, and that those x's that survive to the surface will be phonetically syllabic. The major processes by which x's are deleted are the OCR (which is universal) and both subsidiary onset creation rules (creating onset clusters) and the MCR's, i.e. margin creation rules, that create "closed weight units", whether closed by a single [+cons] or by a margin cluster. If a WU is not affected by any x-deletion rule, it will be syllabic.

A particularly interesting subclass of such WU's concern consonant segments which, in a language with syllables, do not belong to any syllable. Clements and Keyser (1983), for instance, consider words such as knish and Pnom (Penh) to have an initial extrasyllabic consonant. In the weight tier framework, these words would have the corresponding representations in (69).

(69)

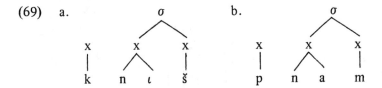

In (69) we see that the initial consonant, which does not belong to the single syllable of these words nevertheless has a WU of its own. The reason why it cannot join that syllable is that the onset–adjunction rules of English will disallow stop + nasal sequences (e.g. *[bnɪk]).[16] As further support for their analysis, Clements and Keyser note that a short epenthetic

schwa may optionally be inserted to realize these consonants, i.e. [kᵊnɪš],
[pᵊnam]. In their framework one would presumably first determine the
syllabification and then insert optionally a V unit with schwa features. In
my framework, the schwa is inserted to associate with the WU of the extrasyllabic consonant, yielding the optional variants of (69) given in (70).

(70)   a.   b.

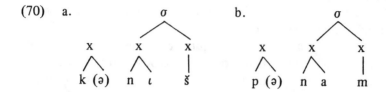

We do this after the syllable formation rules have ceased to apply since
the C + schwa sequence does not constitute a syllable in its own right. It
does, however, constitute a WU, as can be seen. Again we see that we may
have something which is [+syll] without constituting a syllable! Going
back to (69), then, extrasyllabic consonants which remain extrasyllabic
to the surface will thus necessarily be interpreted as carrying weight,
hence as being [+syll]. The examples given involve obstruents which thus
may be weight–bearing (syllabic) to the very end. We will see further examples of this in the discussion of Berber in section 5.4.

There may also be extrasyllabic consonants at the end of a word. This
is probably the way to think of the "appendix" recognized for German
by Halle and Vergnaud (1980), who propose that certain [+cor] consonants are not actually part of the syllable margin, but occur outside it.
Halle and Vergnaud would thus have the representation of (des) Herbsts
'of the autumn' in (71a), while I would represent the same word as in
(71b).

(71)   a.   σ   b.

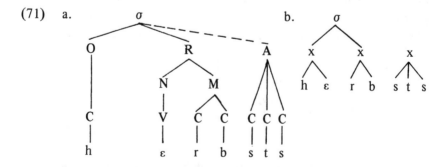

It is not clear whether the appendix would necessarily be a constituent of
the syllable in (71a) at the same level as the onset and rime, or whether
it has a different status. In (71b) I have assumed that the three extrasyllabic consonants -sts somehow come to share a single WU, though

this is not crucial. Probably a similar analysis is called for in English, as seen in the representations in (72).

(72)   a.

The careful pronunciation of tests is given in (72a). There I suggest that the final -ts belongs to an extrasyllabic WU. (It is not crucial that the -t be extrasyllabic, although it is essential that the -s be so analyzed.) The casual speech variant [tɛṣs] is represented in (72b) as one syllabified -s followed by an identical extrasyllabic -s. The latter has its own beat, i.e. its own rearticulation, which is predicted by the WU which remains intact. It is hard to demonstrate that the final [s] in (72b) is extrasyllabic. It may be that its rearticulation with a separate beat is predictable simply from the extra x that does not undergo an MCR. What makes the extra-syllabic hypothesis attractive, as in the case of the "appendix" in Halle and Vergnaud's analysis of German, is that the syllable structure is still preserved: the syllabified portion of (72b) adheres to the generalizations of English syllable structure, whereas the inclusion of the second [s] within the syllable in (72b) would create an unacceptable consonant cluster. Now it may be that such constraints are satisfied at an earlier level only and that extrasyllabicity is irrelevant. This seems, however, a fruit-ful area for further research.[17]

Chapter 5

Segments without Weight

In the previous section it was seen that syllabicity can exist without syllable structure, and that there may be extrasyllabic segments even in languages where syllable structure is attested. In this section I shall discuss cases where segments exist without any WU. Two separate situations will be distinguished: (a) cases where the weightless segment is underlying; and (b) cases where the weightless segment is epenthetic. I shall claim that phonetic epenthesis (a) is related to the structure of WU's, not syllables (as has often been claimed) and (b) *never* involves insertion of a WU, only the insertion of segmental (or other) features.

5.1. Underlying weightless consonants

In this section I will discuss cases where there is reason to posit underlying segments without corresponding weight units. I begin with the familiar examples from French in (73).

(73) a. petit [pəti]   'little (m)'
      b. petit garçon [pəti garsɔ̃]   'little boy'
      c. petit ami [pətit ami]   'little friend (m.)'
      d. petite [pətit]   'little (f.)'

As seen in (73), there are certain final consonants in French, mostly [+cor], which are only pronounced if there is a following vowel. The final /t/ of petit 'little (m)' is not pronounced in (73a) because it is followed by pause and it is not pronounced in (73b) because it is followed by a consonant. It is pronounced in (73c) because it is followed by a vowel (within the same phonological phrase). In (73d) we see that even the silent schwa in petite 'little (f.)' satisfies the criterion so that the /t/ may be pronounced.

Most accounts follow Schane (1968) in postulating underlying final consonants which are subject to a consonant deletion (but cf. Tranel 1981). Recently Clements and Keyser (1983) have treated these final "latent" consonants as extrasyllabic, as seen in (74).

(74)   a.

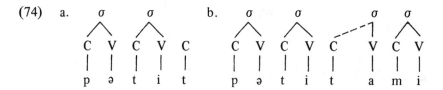

Recall that Clements and Keyser propose a flat syllable structure. In (74a) we have two CV syllables followed by a C which is not syllabified. This extrasyllabicity is indicated as a lexical feature on this word. In (74b), the extrasyllabicity is not observed since the final C of petit can become the onset of a CV syllable with the vowel of the following syllable constituting its nucleus, as shown. Since Clements and Keyser have proposed elsewhere that an extrasyllabic consonant may in another language (e.g. English) be pronounced, though variable, as in the case of [knɪš-kᵊnɪš], either languages will vary in how they treat extrasyllabic material (i.e. either pronouncing it or not pronouncing it), or its pronounceability depends upon whether the extrasyllabic material is *pre*-syllabic (as in the case of knish) or *post*-syllabic (as in the case of petit). With so little work having been done on extrasyllabicity, it seems premature to assert anything more than the variation we have just seen in English vs. French.

I would like, however, to tentatively take a strong position and say that within the WU framework extrasyllabic material is always pronounced. That is, there is no program for "skipping over" unsyllabified material in any language. This position is made possible by the fact that this framework also recognizes "floating" segments (i.e. those not having a WU) as distinct from segments which have a WU, but which for one reason or another do not get incorporated into a syllable. I will therefore propose that the final /t/ of petit is instead a weightless consonant, as seen in (75a).

(75)   a.

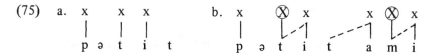

The underlying representation of this word in (75a) includes a final segment /t/ without any WU as well as a schwa without a WU (see section 5.2). The correct output [pəti] is obtained in (75a) by applying the OCR to the /ti/ sequence and by associating the weightless schwa to the WU of the preceding consonant. Since the MCR joins a [+cons] segment to the WU of a preceding [-cons] segment only if the former has a (to be deleted) WU of its own, it will not apply in (75a). Thus, the final floating /t/ will not be pronounced in this form.

In (75b) we see that the weightless /t/ automatically becomes the onset of the following WU by a reapplication of the OCR post-lexically.

This raises the question of whether the OCR in either its lexical or post-lexical application should be formulated as requiring that the [+cons] segment start out with a WU of its own. If not, then the OCR may be reformulated as in (76).

(76)
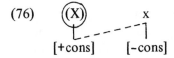

[+cons]   [−cons]

If we reformulate the OCR as in (76) then an important prediction will be made. This prediction is that a weightless consonant may be exceptional only with respect to margin-creation, not with respect to onset-creation. In other words, we do not expect a weightless consonant to appear as in (77), where it has failed to become the onset of the following [−cons] WU:

(77)   *   x   (→   x   )
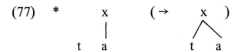

         t   a   t   a

The representation in (77) would automatically become a single CV WU. In the CV approach, with extrasyllabicity, it would have to be stipulated that extrasyllabic C's must not be exceptions to the CV syllable creation rule, which is taken to be universal, e.g. Steriade's (1982) "CV linking" procedure. Clements and Keyser would have to refer to the "universality" of the CV linking rule within word formation and the non−universality of the syllable adjunction rule creating margins in French. In this account speakers would have to have some meta−awareness of what is universal and cannot be violated, whereas in my account this non−exceptionality is directly incorporated into the forms of the rules in question. The OCR rule in (76) allows for weightless [+cons] segments, as well as weighted ones. The corresponding MCR in French would, on the other hand, specify that the [+cons] must have a WU in order to join the preceding WU in forming a CVC unit. Let us assume that this unit is a single WU. The MCR would therefore be as in (78).

(78)   x   Ⓧ⁾
           ┌────────┘
        [−cons]   [+cons]

This rule requires two WU's in its input. Thus, the weightless /t/ in (75a) may not undergo this (language−specific) rule.

There is a lengthy literature on the significance of floating tones for autosegmental theory (see, for example, Leben 1973 and Goldsmith 1976a,b, among others). We know that tones may "float", i.e. that they may be present in underlying representations without having any syllabic support. In my system this would simply mean without having any WU. Now the proposal I have just made for French, and which can be generalized to other similar situations (e.g. the famous Maori case of Hale (1973) and Kiparsky (1973)), is exactly parallel: in (75a) we have a "floating consonant". In other words, there is a complete segmental representation, but no WU. There is also the possibility of an incomplete segmental representation. The example that comes to mind is also from French. In (79) I contrast Clements and Keyser's account of French h-aspiré with its translation into WU phonology:

(79)   a.   b.

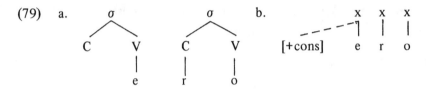

The word in question is héros 'hero' [ero] which among other things does not allow the definite article le to syllabify onto its initial vowel to form a CV syllable. We thus obtain le héros [lə ero] and not *l'héros [lero]. As seen in (79a), Clements and Keyser propose an empty C on the CV tier to block the enjambement of a preceding consonant. This is, then, the counterpart to Anderson's (1982) empty V slot for the schwa in French. In my account in (79b), I have a floating [+cons] which accomplishes the same thing as the empty C. Note that I do not need a WU, though it would automatically have been deleted by the OCR. By the same token, Clements and Keyser have no need to refer to the dummy C on their CV tier as extrasyllabic, since it cannot be pronounced without further features anyway. The fact that the [+cons] specification may function on its own in (79b) points to the special status of this feature, something which is returned to in section 9.

5.2. Underlying weightless vowels

Now that we have seen cases of "floating consonants" the question arises as to whether vowels may float. In a system whereby there necessarily is syllable structure and syllables are necessarily projected from each vowel, this would not be possible. However, I have assumed neither the first nor the second principle as universal, and in fact, cases of floating vowels are found just as readily as the consonant cases.

A case of vowel weightlessness can be made for the Russian yers, which I represent, following Pesetsky (1979), as I and U. These "fleeting vowels" are either realized with their vowel height lowered or they are "deleted". The major generalization is that these vowels will be realized (in their lowered form) if followed by a consonant followed by another yer. If followed by a consonant and a non-yer vowel, the yer will not be realized.[18] An example is given in (80).

(80) a.
  'forehead' (nom.)

  b.
  'forehead' (gen.)

In (80a), because it is followed by another yer, the weightless vowel /U/ associates onto the WU of the preceding consonant. In (80b), however, where the following vowel is a non-yer, /U/ is not realized (and presumably skipped over, since it is not attached to the core, or deleted). The rule of yer-association is formalized in (81).

(81)
  [+cons] [−cons] [+cons]

This rule refers crucially to the non-branching characteristic of the following consonantal WU, as indicated. This WU will branch only if the following vowel input has its own WU, as in (80b), in which case the [+cons] [−cons] sequence will undergo the OCR. There is, thus, considerable advantage to be reaped from allowing vowels also to be weightless in underlying representations.

A second case where I would like to propose weightless vowel representations comes from Chuvash. As cited in section 1, the reduced vowels /ă/ are /ĕ/ skipped over in stress placement. According to Krueger (1961: 86), stress is carried by the last full vowel of a word, as in /kálăttămăr/ 'we would say'. In languages where the crucial vowel distinction is between long and short or between tense and lax, the opposition of one vs. two WU's would be appropriate. It would not be very satisfactory here, though, to propose that all full vowels are geminates, while the two reduced vowels are single.

Instead, I propose that reduced vowels are weightless and that full vowels have one WU, i.e. they are regular, single length vowels. This gives us the representation of 'we would say' in (82).

(82)
  k a l a t a m a r

In this example, all but the first vowel are reduced and hence weightless. There is one application of the OCR to produce a branching WU. I therefore propose that the rule be formulated as stressing "the last branching WU of a word", as in (83):

(83)   x → [+stress] / ___ Q ## (where Q does not contain $\underset{\wedge}{x}$)

The formulation in (83) makes the prediction by virtue of Halle and Vergnaud's "Q variable" notation that if a word contains only reduced vowels, as in (84), the first of these will receive the stress:

(84)   tắtămăr   'we got up'

The claim made explicit in (83) is that it is the WU's which carry stress in Chuvash, not syllables. It may be that this will have to be modified somewhat in light of the fact that stress is a feature on *syllables*. Where a language assigns accent to units smaller than the syllable, i.e. to moras, we normally have a "pitch-accent" or "tonal accent" language, e.g. Japanese, Classical Greek, Somali etc. Thus, an alternative that might ultimately be more viable typologically is to have syllable formation sensitive to the full vs. reduced contrast, still represented as a single WU vs. no WU. We would first construct syllables on the basis of the x'ed in [−cons] segments, then assign stress to the "last syllable of the word", followed then by the rule in (85), which assigns the weightless vowels /ă/ and /ĕ/ to the WU of the preceding consonant:

(85)   x
         ┌─ ─ ─ ─
      [+cons]   [−cons]

This rule would thus apply to the three weightless vowels in (82) *after* the stress placement rule applies. This view of gradual weighting and syllabification processes pervades the approach taken here. At an early stage a segment has weight, only to lose it later. At an early stage a segment doesn't have weight, only to gain it later. It is the *ordering* of the rules which can account for the complex cases. The yers and the reduced vowels of Chuvash start out as weightless and therefore cannot feed the initial syllable formation process of the language. Later, when they acquire weight (through rule (85)) they then go on to create syllables. This is, of course, assuming that languages such as Chuvash really have syllables.

   A third case concerns the analysis of schwa in French, an issue which has attracted much attention in the phonological literature (see Anderson

1982 and references cited therein). Anderson analyzes French schwa as an empty vowel nucleus. Assuming that this means a featureless V on the CV tier, and assuming the flat syllable structure of Clements and Keyser (1983) instead of the hierarchical syllable found in Anderson's study, a word such as pelouse 'lawn' would be represented as in (86a).

(86) a.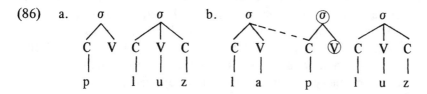

A default vowel spelling rule will introduce the phonetic features of schwa in (86a) to derive [pəluz]. In (86b), on the other hand, it is observed, according to Anderson, that when a vowel precedes a consonant + empty V sequence, the consonant joins the preceding (now closed) syllable, and the empty V is deleted. The rule which thus derives la pǿlouse 'the lawn' is formalized by Anderson as in (87).

(87)   V]$_\sigma$ # [$_\sigma$ C Ø]
        1   2   3   4   →   1 2 3]$_\sigma$ [$_\sigma$ 4]

However, there is some question as to the correctness of the syllable division in Anderson's [lap·luz]. Rialland (in press) tests this claim by considering pairs of forms which by rule (87) should turn out to be homophonous. She points out, for instance, that the "stranded" [r] in (88a) is phonetically both longer and of greater intensity than its counterpart in (88b).

(88) a. le bas r(e)trouvé hier   [lə ba r̩ truve yɛr]   'the stocking re-
                                                          covered yesterday'
      b. le bar trouvé hier   [lə bar truve yɛr]   'the bar found
                                                          yesterday'

While it is possible, particularly in fast speech, for the two phrases in (88) to become homophonous, they are for many speakers distinct and must therefore receive different representations even when the schwa is lacking in (88a). The different representations that are needed are available within the WU framework. In (89) we see appropriate representations of the relevant forms bas retrouvé and bar trouvé.

(89) a.   x   x   x   x   b.   x   x   x
          /\ | /|\   /\   /|\   /|\   /\
         b a   r ə   t r u v e   b a r   t r u   v e

All of the segments in (89a,b) have an underlying x except the schwa in (89a). The forms given in (89) are those obtained after the application of the OCR, the onset adjunction rule (which adds the t to the following x and deletes its x), and the MCR (adding the r to the preceding WU in (89b) and deleting its x) The schwa in (89a) is prevented from associating to the preceding WU of the r, since this in turn is preceded by a vowel. A late deletion of the weightless schwa will predict that in (89a) the r is "syllabic", i.e. the most sonorous segment dominated by its weight unit. However, it is not syllabic in (89b), where the vowel a, associated onto the same WU, is more sonorous. This difference accounts, then, for the acoustic discrepancy between the two forms reported by Rialland.

In (89a) the two consonants found in sequence (rt) have the more sonorous one preceding the less sonorous one. Rialland also contrasts forms where the more sonorous consonant *follows* the less sonorous one, as in (90).

(90)   a.   je l(e) f(e)rai   [žlə fɾɛ]   'I will do it'
        b.   c'est à ses frais   [sɛta sɛ frɛ]   'it's at his/her expense'

The sequence in question is fr. If the difference between (90a) and (90b) were parallel to that observed in (88a) vs. (88b), we would expect there to be durational and intensity differences in the two f's. That is, we would expect the deletion of schwa in (90a) to affect the preceding consonant, as it does in (88a). The reverse is true, however. The r in (90a) is both longer and of greater intensity than its counterpart in (90b). I propose the derivation of the relevant part [lə fɾɛ] as in (91)

(91)   a.      b.

In (91a) there are two weightless schwas in the underlying representation. The first associates onto the preceding [+cons] WU, since this WU is not preceded by a vowel. In the second word, one instance of the OCR is also observed. The second schwa may not associate because once the first schwa has associated, an environment is created which bleeds schwa-association, revealing the well-known left-to-right application of the schwa rule. In (91b) I have deleted the non-associated schwa, leaving a WU dominating the consonant f. Since f is not an ideal consonant to carry syllabicity, and since there is a more sonorous consonant r to its right, the latter extends its association to the left, creating the lengthening (and greater intensity) associated with that consonant in this form.

This having been said, let us return to the underlying representation of pelouse [pəluz] and [la pluz]. As seen in (92a),

(92) a.

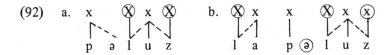

The circled x's are deleted by the OCR and the MCR. The floating schwa must associate, as indicated, because the preceding [+cons] WU is not preceded by a vowel (but see below). In (92b), on the other hand, after the operation of the OCR and the MCR the floating schwa may not associate because the preceding consonant *is* preceded by a vowel. Now, what is crucial about (92b) is that the resulting weighted p is not free to join the WU of the following l by an onset adjunction rule (as would automatically occur in a word such as place 'place'). Thus, the floating schwa serves the important function of blocking onset adjunction. The resulting form in (92b) is realized as is or, apparently in fast speech, the WU of the p may in fact be removed, assigning the p to the preceding WU. (Apparently the l does not associate to the WU of the p, as we saw in (91b)).

The rules affecting schwa are complex, and I have only touched on what I hope is the basis for a solution. The "weighted consonants" that result from the non-realization of schwa are effectively represented within this framework, including cases of "exceptional schwa deletion", as in (93).

(93) a. je m' en vais   [žmã v ɛ]   'I'm leaving
     b. reviens vite   [*r*vyɛ̃ vit]   'come back quick'
     c. petit gars   [*p*ti ga]   'little kid'

The italicized initial consonants all have a WU of their own, accounting for their beat or syllabicity. Thus the *phonetics* of schwa deletion can be more straightforwardly accommodated within this framework than within a framework that commits one to syllables. Two additional facts are explained. First, as pointed out to me by Bernard Tranel, the weightless representation of schwa explains why no French word can begin with schwa: if such a word had an initial schwa, this schwa would never be realized, because it would not have a [+cons] WU to attach to. Second, it provides a different explanation from Anderson's as to why "h-aspiré" may not be followed by schwa. If we represent h-aspiré as floating [+cons], as was proposed in (79), then a həCV sequence would have the representation in (94).

(94)

             Ⓧ   x

   [+cons]   ə   C   V

In this representation only the OCR applies. The schwa may not link with the preceding floating [+cons] because the latter does not have a WU, and the floating [+cons] may not link with the following schwa by the OCR, because the latter also does not have a WU. Thus, the sequence h–aspiré + schwa could have no realization, and is therefore never present as an initial sequence in underlying forms.

Finally, if we maintain that the final t in petit is weightless, as in (75a) above, then it will be necessary to say that the feminine suffix consists of a WU without features, as in (95).

(95)

$$\left[\begin{array}{c} \left[\begin{array}{c} \\ \text{n.f.} \end{array}\left[\begin{array}{cccc} & \overset{\text{x}}{\underset{\text{p}}{|}} & \overset{\text{x}}{\underset{\text{e}}{}} & \overset{\text{x}}{\underset{\text{t}}{|}} \ \overset{\text{x}}{\underset{\text{i}}{|}} & \overset{}{\underset{\text{t}}{}} \end{array}\right]\right]\end{array}\right]^{\text{x}}$$ 'little' (fem.)

n.m.

The MCR may now apply to this form, since this rule requires that the [+cons] segment in question have its own WU. In this connection, note that instead of reformulating the OCR as in (76), it may be that the reapplication of the "OCR" post-lexically would simply associate a [+cons] onto a following [–cons] WU, whether the [+cons] were floating or whether it were the margin of the preceding WU. Thus, rather than a deletion of its WU in the latter case, it simply would deassociate. We then would have the following derivation of petite amie in (96).

(96)   a.   b.

(96a) shows the operation of the OCR and the MCR. (96b) shows that the margin consonant associates onto the following [–cons] WU, disassociating from its own WU. I leave open the question of whether feminine forms have an underlying schwa as well as an underlying featureless WU.

5.3. Epenthetic consonants

In the preceding section we saw that a language may have either or both weightless consonants or vowels at the underlying level. In this and the following section we shall see that epenthetic consonants and epenthetic vowels are also weightless, though they, of course, do not exist in underlying representations. In this section we first consider epenthetic consonants.

Gokana is a language rich in epenthetic segments. In (49) I presented a rule epenthesizing [i] between underlying [+cons] segments within the foot. In (42) a rule of glottal stop epenthesis was formalized which, with certain modifications, is found in numerous languages of the world which require such a [+cons] onset on stems, words or phrases, e.g. German, Arabic etc. It is significant that both of these epenthetic segments are introduced *without a WU*. I will propose here that phonetic epenthesis *never* introduces a WU, only a segmental matrix (whether completely or incomplete specified). The theoretical consequences of this move are discussed in section 5.5.

Gokana has two other cases of consonant epenthesis which will be illustrated. In Hyman (1982a) alternations such as those in (97) were discussed:

(97) a.   oò tu-i   'you pl. took'   oò gɔ̄-ĩ   'you pl. hid'
      b.   oò zov-ii   'you pl. danced   oò bān-ĩ ĩ   'you pl. begged'
      c.   oò sii-rii   'you pl. caught'   oò nāā-nĩ ĩ   'you pl. made'

The column on the left involves the oral verb toots /tú/ 'take', /Zob/ 'dance' and /síi/ 'catch', while the column on the right involves the nasal verbs roots /gɔ̄/ 'hide', /bāD/ 'beg' and /Dāa/ 'make'. The underlying forms are justified in section 8.1 below, superceding Hyman (1982b). In the latter study it was argued that nasality should be represented as [+NAS] on a separate autosegmental tier. The suffix in (97) does not have any specification for nasality, but takes its nasality either from a [+NAS] to the left, or becomes [-NAS] as the default, unmarked value of this feature. The archisegments /B, V, D, Z, G/ are realized [b, v, l, z, g] when the nasal tier is [-NAS], but as [m, ɱ, n,ɲ, ŋ] when the nasal tier is [+NAS] . The [-NAS] archisegments /B/ and /D/ are realized instead as [v] and [r], when occurring intervocalically, as in the left column of (97b) and (97c). In (98) we see that the logophoric suffix /ÈÈ/ has similar alternations to the second person plural subject suffix:

(98) a.   oò tu-è   'he₁ took'   oò gɔ̄-ɛ̀   'he₁ hid'
      b.   oò zov-èè   'he₁ danced'   oò bān-ɛ̀ɛ̀   'he₁ begged'
      c.   oò sii-rèè   'he₁ caught'   oò nāā-nɛ̀ɛ̀   'he₁ made

In both (97a) and (98a) the suffix in question is realized as a short vowel after another short vowel. This is obtained through the DGR formalized in (25). In (97b) and (98b) the underlying geminate vowel is observed after a consonant-final verb root. Finally, in (97c) and (98c), we observe that there is a consonant [r] or [n] appearing between a verb root ending in a geminate vowel and either of these two suffixes. A rule of D-epenthesis is thus required, as formulated in (99).

(99)

This rule inserts "D" (the archiphoneme realized as oral [r] intervocalically or as nasal [n]) whenever within the foot there is a succession
of geminate vowels. As seen, this "D" is associated to the first WU of the
second geminate, forming its onset.[19] As in the GS epenthesis rule in (42),
only the segmental features are epenthesized - i.e. there is no WU accompanying the "D" in (99). The claim implicit in this approach is that epenthetic segments make other WU's pronounceable - thus, unlike most
approaches to epenthesis, I do not make the assumption that epenthesis
is related to syllable structure - at least, not directly.

A further justification for this last point comes from cases where it
is unclear whether it is a full segment that is being inserted. Consider the
alternate pronunciations of the following Gokana words:

(100) a. /síi + a/   →   [sííá]   ~   [síí^{y}á]   'catch' (intr.)
           /bùu + a/   →   [bùùà]   ~   [bùù^{w}à]   'uproot' (intr.)

In an earlier discussion it was stated that Gokana does not have glides.
This was a slight misstatement. As seen in the second transcription of
the two verb forms in (100), a "slight homorganic glide" is sometimes
heard in these and comparable forms. This glide is possible only when the
preceding vowel is both [+high] and geminate and is seen in the above
forms where the verb roots 'catch' and 'uproot' are followed by the toneless intransitive suffix /-a/. Rather than having to insert a glide, we provide
for the optional linking of the [-cons, +high] matrix with the following
[-cons] WU, as seen in (101).

(101) a.   b.

The fact that the epenthetic glide "isn't quite a consonant" is nicely accounted for by this optional additional association.[20]

Notice that this kind of analysis is required for a number of languages.
For example, in Aghem (Hyman 1979), /C$\frac{1}{1}$a/ sequences are frequently
pronounced [C$\frac{1}{1}^\gamma$a], e.g. [k$\frac{1}{1}$-b$\frac{1}{1}^\gamma$á] 'leopard'. Since there is even evidence
of a tonal nature that /$\frac{1}{1}$a/ must be treated as a single vowel, i.e. as a single
WU, it is theoretically impossible for the insertion of the gamma–glide to
involve the weight tier (or a corresponding CV tier) in this language. Recall in this context my discussion (Hyman 1975:191) of Gudschinsky,
Popovich and Popovich's (1970) syllable derivations repeated in (102).

(102) a. /CiC/ → CiəC → CiyəC
b. /CoC/ → CoəC → CowəC
c. /Cɬ C/ → Cɬ əC → Cɬ γəC
d. /Cɬ C/ → Cɬ əC → Cɬ γə̄C → Cɬ ŋ ə̄C

Here we observe both schwa-diphthongization and insertion of a glide
homorganic to the preceding vowel. (The final line of (102d) has the
gamma-glide nasalizing to a [ŋ], something which also happens in Aghem.) In light of the preceding discussion and the view taken here of
epenthesis, my 1975 comments on resyllabification in Maxakali may
have been unwarranted. In any case, the motivation for this approach to
epenthesis, developed in section 5.5 below, suggests that many statements
on epenthetic processes in different languages may require reevaluation.

5.4. Epenthetic Vowels

In this section I shall give a brief discussion of vowel epenthesis in a
single language, Berber (Tamazight dialect). This language has been the
subject of a number of excellent studies including Saib (1976a,b), Guerssel
(1978) and for the most detailed account, Penchoen (1973). Underlyingly, Berber has only the three underlying vowels /i, u, a/. On the surface, however, there is a fourth vowel, a schwa, whose occurrence is completely predictable, as seen in the verb forms in (103).

(103) a. /xdm + x/ → [xə ðməx] 'I work'
b. /t + xdm/ → [θəxðəm] 'you sg.f. work'
c. /xdm+ n/ → [xə ðmən] 'they m. work'

As seen, I assume that the verb root /xdm/ 'work' has no underlying vowel
(and also that non-strident fricatives are underlyingly non-geminate
stops). In a segmental account, the rule required to insert schwa is as
formulated for "abstract analysis A" by Saib (1976a:127) in (104).

$$(104) \quad \emptyset \rightarrow \text{ə} \; / \; \{ \#, C \} \underline{\quad} \left\{ \begin{matrix} \# \\ C \end{matrix} \right\}$$

This rule is designed to apply right-to-left within a word, starting by inserting a schwa before a word-final consonant which itself is preceded
either by a word boundary or another consonant. In some cases the location of the schwas do not exactly follow what is predicted by rule (104),
but these cases can be handled by subsidiary rules or conditions (see
below).

Looking at the forms in (103), we see that each verb form undergoes
two applications of rule (104). Thus, the underlying sequence of four
consonants becomes on the surface [CəCCəC].

A potential problem arises, however, when the number of consonants in sequence is an odd number, as in (105).

(105) *Saib*   *Penchoen*
   a. /xdm/ → ə x ðəm   xðəm   'work'
   b. /n + xdm + m/ → ə nxə ðməm   nxə ðməm   'we work'
   c. /t + xdm + m/ → ə θxə ðməm   θxə ðməm   'you pl.m. work'

Saib's rule in (104) predicts that there will be a schwa before a word-initial sequence of two consonants, and he transcribes forms such as in (105) with an initial schwa. Penchoen, on the other hand, does not transcribe a schwa word-initially, as can be seen from his tables of verb paradigms (1973:96-99), where he provides transcriptions of some detail. The truth, I believe, falls somewhere in between. It is clear that the word-initial consonants in (105) do not form a complex onset with the following consonant. Berber, like most Arabic dialects does not normally allow complex onsets. Thus, the initial consonants in (105), not being onsets, still have their WU's. They are, then essentially syllabic, since they have weight. This confirms my own impression, having heard such forms pronounced in Tamazight. The rule in (104) should, I believe, therefore be modified so that schwa's will not be inserted word initially. This is true even in a case such as (106), where there is a geminate consonant appearing word-initially without a schwa :

(106) /ttbddl/ → [ttβəddəl] 'to change'

Both units of the geminate are in a pre-onset position, and there is a strong tendency to degeminate in this position (leaving a short stop, which still contrasts with single /t/, which is pronounced [θ]).

   The WU framework provides a satisfactory account of schwa insertion, which is accomplished via the rule in (107).

(107)

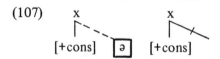

This rule says that a schwa is inserted and associated with a [+cons] WU when the latter is followed by another [+cons] WU which does not branch. The reason for the non-branching condition on the rule is that we do not want to insert a schwa between the /k/ and the /s/ in /aksum/ 'meat'. Because this word has an underlying vowel /u/ in it, the OCR will first create a branching weight unit -su- and the non-branching condition in (107) will block the rule from applying.

The rule in (107) is, I believe, superior to the way the rule would be stated in either a segmental account or with a CV tier (see the next section for the consequences this rule has for the non–separability of geminates). The rule still applies from right to left, but there is no need to refer to word boundaries – *and* the anomalous nature of word–initial consonant clusters is account for.[21] Penchoen describes a number of other alternatives, some of which Saib also discusses, involving cases where the schwa does not appear where the rule would predict. One straightforward case concerns word–final /t, tt, ṭṭ/ which are not separated from a preceding consonant by a schwa:

(108) a. /t + xdm + m + t/   →   [θxəðməmθ]   'you pl.f. work'
       b. /xdm + n + t/   →   [xəðmənθ]   'they f. work'

A comparison with (105c) and (104b) will reveal that the final /t/ consonant is a feminine suffix which, as also seen, clusters with the preceding consonant. Compare for the same cluster the following masculine/feminine noun pairs:

(109) a. aɣɣul   'jackass'   θaɣulθ   'jenny'
       b. asərðun   'mule'   θasərðunθ   'she–mule'
       c. afus   'hand'   θafusθ   'small hand'

In the WU framework, one could either mark off the WU of word final /t/, so that it would not count in establishing the placement of schwa by rule (107), or one could precede (107) with a "readjustment rule", a kind of MCR, adjoining the /t/ to the WU of the preceding consonant and deleting the WU of the /t/. Certain other cases where the schwa does not appear where (107) predicts would have to do with similar readjustments taking place prior to the application of schwa insertion. In at least one case which Penchoen discusses (p. 95), we are dealing instead with a late or fast speech deletion of schwa:

(110) /t + sɣ + d/   →   [θəsɣəð]   →   [θsɣəð]   'you sg. buy'

Rule (107) inserts two schwas, as seen, the first of which can optionally delete in fast speech. The reason we know that it was there is because /t/ does not spirantize before /s/, e.g. /t + sɣ/ 'she buys' is pronounced [tsəɣ]. Thus, schwa is first inserted, then /t/ spirantizes, then schwa is deleted – but only in fast speech.

A different kind of problem arises in words involving sonorants which sometimes have alternate pronunciations. A verb such as /ns/ 'to wear' is pronounced by some as [nəs] (as predicted by (107)), but by others as

[əns]. Saib discusses the early scholars of Berber who attempted to predict these schwas in taking account of the relative sonority of the consonants involved. A full account goes well beyond the purposes of this
section. I shall therefore address only one point made by Penchoen (1973:
94), who states that when a schwa is inserted between a consonant and a
sonorant, instead of a real schwa being observed on the surface, the
sonorant is realized as syllabic. By sonorant he includes /m, n, r, ṛ, l, y, w,
mm, nn, rr, ṛṛ, ll/, i.e. single and geminate nasals and liquids and single
glides (whose geminates, being /gg/ and /ggʷ/, are not sonorant). In other
words, Penchoen transcribes /i + xdm/ 'he works' and /i + kkr/ 'he stands
up' as ⁻[ixðm̩] and [ikkṛ], respectively. His statement on p. 94 seems to
be at odds with another statement on p.10, at least as concerns the glides
/y/ and /w/. On p. 10 he states that schwa + /y/ is realized [iy] and schwa
+ /w/ is realized [uw], though these may simplify to [i] and [u] in fast
speech. Thus, /bby/ 'cut' (perf. stem) is realized [bbiy] in normal speech
(merging with /bbiy/ 'cut' (perf. neg. stem)), but as [bbi] in rapid speech.
It is significant for my analysis of word-initial clusters that in this position his /y/ and /w/ vocalize to [i] and [u], respectively, e.g. /yša/ 'he gave'
is pronounced [iša]. If a real schwa had been inserted as per Saib's rule,
we would expect at least as a variant the form *[iyša].

We thus can exclude the glides from Penchoen's observation on syllabic
sonorants and assume that they take a real schwa which assimilates to the
glide and which may, in fast speech, be accompanied by the loss of the
glide. The question about such forms as [ixðm̩] is whether a schwa has
been inserted and then deleted, leaving behind a syllabic sonorant, or
whether the schwa was not inserted in the first place. I have not been
able to find any way to choose between these two possibilities. I will
therefore note that if there is reason not to insert a schwa before a nasal
or liquid, this can be accomplished simply by mending rule (107) as
follows:

(107′)

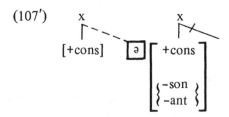

This rule now says that the schwa will be inserted and associated onto a
[+cons] WU when the following non-branching [+cons] WU is either an
obstruent or is [−ant]. (I am assuming that /ṛ/ and /ṛṛ/ are [−ATR],
but still [+ant].) Thus, a form such as /tṛ/ 'to go down' is pronounced
[ðṛ], with no epenthesis. I assume that if (107′) is adopted there will

be a need to associate the pre-sonorant consonant onto the sonorant's WU (a kind of onset-creation), deleting the WU of the former. This complication would be offset by the non-necessity of a schwa–deletion rule before sonorant consonants (cf. my remarks in section 9, however).

5.5. Generalizations and predictions

One of the striking results of the above analyses of underlying weightless segments and epenthetic segments is the extent to which one can talk about these processes without reference to the syllable. Instead of preferred syllable structures, there are preferred WU structures, e.g. a WU at the beginning of a grammatical unit (stem, word, phrase) should begin with a [+cons] specification; if not present in the lexical representation, a glottal stop is frequently epenthesized, as we have seen. The schwa insertion rule of Berber has also been stated without reference to the syllable. Whether Berber goes on to construct syllables is, I believe, an open question. There is relatively little evidence for syllables in Tamazight, especially since there is no word stress. Thus, the question that arises is whether everything can be done in Berber (and other languages) with WU's and if so, just when and where is the syllable required by (other) languages?

In this section I would like to develop the consequences of the above view of epenthesis. It will be recalled that I made the claim that epenthesis never adds an x to the WU tier. The correlate in a CV tier approach would be that epenthetic segments do not have a C or V on the core, though this has not, to my knowledge, ever been explored as a possibility. There are at least three consequences of the approach to epenthesis I am advocating, all making predictions that are, as far as I know, exceptionless.

(a) If epenthesis does not involve the insertion of a WU, it will never be possible for an epenthetic consonant to separate a geminate vowel, or for an epenthetic vowel to separate a geminate consonant. The fact that a schwa may not be inserted between the two length units of a geminate consonant in Berber has been discussed by Saib (1976a), Guerssel (1978) and Steriade (1982), among others. Thus, underlying /bdd/ 'to stand up' is pronounced [βədd], not *[βðəð]. Given my representation in (111) and rule (107), this is the only possible result:

$$(111) \quad x \quad x \quad x \quad \rightarrow \quad x \quad x \quad x$$

The same is true of derivations such as in note 21. So, the prediction is made that true geminates are not broken up by epenthetic segments, and this prediction appears to hold true.[22]

(b) If epenthetic processes are not allowed to insert WU's then it should be impossible to have an epenthetic geminate consonant or an epenthetic geminate vowel. Such a case could not be readily accomodated by this approach and would therefore be a strong counterexample to the theory. (We *may* however speak of a lengthening process as the insertion of a WU without a segmental matrix, e.g. the phrase-final lengthening rule in ChiMwi:ni (Kisseberth and Abasheikh 1974). Such rules are not usually referred to as processes of epenthesis, however.)

(c) A third consequence of the weightless nature of epenthetic segments is that features may be epenthesized *on one tier at a time only*. What this means is that one does not insert a feature matrix on the one hand accompanied by an autosegment on a different tier. Thus, there are no cases known to me where a language with a nasal tier epenthesizes a [+NAS] segment. Epenthetic consonants are always oral (unmarked), and where there appears to be an addition of a nasal segment, something else is in reality taking place. Thus, if a language has a nasal tier and converts /ṼC/ into ṼNC, I would represent this as in (112).

(112)

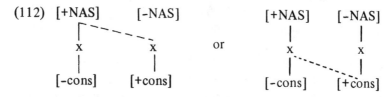

Similarly, languages such as Akan or Igbo with an ATR tier do not epenthesize vowels with a prespecified value for [ATR]. Epenthetic vowels in languages with vowel harmony simply harmonize. What this means, then, is that there is *no opaque epenthesis*. This is predicted by the theory, since an opaque epenthesis, requiring features on two tiers, would have to have a WU as the mediator of the features – but, I have claimed, there is no added WU in "epenthesis".

The clearest example comes from tone languages. I know of no tone language where a vowel is epenthesized with a specified tone. Instead, such epenthetic vowels typically take their tone from the surroundings. There is no a priori reason why this should be the case. For example, one could imagine that a language borrowing words with unacceptable consonant clusters might follow the strategy of inserting an epenthetic vowel with low tone. I know no such example. Instead, consider the adaptation of Hausa words by Nupe speakers illustrated in (113).

(113)		*Hausa*		*Nupe*	
a.	àlhé:rì:	>	àlhērì ~ àlɩ́hērì	'kindness'
b.	àlbárkà:	>	àlbárɩ́kā ~ àlʊ̀bárɩ́kā	'blessing'
c.	àlbàrûs	>	àlbàrû ~ àlʊ̀bàrû	'gunpowder'

The epenthetic vowels are italicized. As seen, there is some variation in how Hausa words are pronounced in Nupe. What is important for us, as I pointed out in Hyman (1970b), is that the [+high] vowel which Nupes insert (generally [i], but [u] before a labial consonant and occasionally [a] before /h/), does not have a constant tone. Nupes do not, for example, insert a high vowel with, say, a M tone, which one might argue to be unmarked in a three tone language (Maddieson 1970, Pulleyblank 1983). Instead, the vowel takes the same tone as the preceding vowel. Two instances of this are seen in the longer variant of (113b), in our terms:

(114)

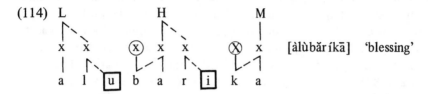

[àlùbăríkā] 'blessing'

As seen in (114), the L and H tones associate onto the epenthetic high vowels to their right. The only further tonal modification required, as seen in the phonetic form, is a L-spreading rule which takes place in a L-H sequence which has a [+voice] consonant intervening (Smith 1967, George 1970). If the intervening consonant is [-voice], L-spreading does not take place, as in [àlìkáwòlī] (< Hausa àlká:wàrí:) 'promise'.

In tone languages, then, we do not expect epenthetic vowels to have a tone of their own. This fact is captured by WU phonology in a principled way, since the WU tier is not available for epenthesis and hence for epenthesis to involve more than one tier. While it might make sense to exclude epenthetic segments with a feature on either a tonal, nasal or ATR tier on the functional grounds that such specified segments would be more "marked", and marked segments should not be available for epenthesis, the view of epenthesis presented here gives a formal explanation for this functional argument.

It will be noted that there are cases that could be argued to involve epenthetic vowels carrying a specified tone, but all of these, to my knowledge, reduce to the kind of morphological processes mentioned in note 22. For example, in Nupe we have the following partially reduplicated gerundives deriving from verbs:

(115) a. /tí/   'screech' → tī-tí   'screeching'
       b. /tē/   'break'   → tī-tē   'breaking'
       c. /tá/   'tell'   → tī-tá   'telling'
       d. /tú/   'ride'   → tū-tú   'riding'
       e. /tò/   'loosen'   → tū-tò   'loosening'

While the situation is somewhat more complicated than this (see Hyman 1970a and the forms in Banfield's (1914) dictionary, which indicate some variation due in part to the nature of the stem-initial consonant), the general rule is that the reduplicated prefix consists of a copy of the stem consonant plus a [+high] vowel agreeing in backness and roundness with the roundness of the stem vowel, i.e. [i] if the stem vowel is /i, e, a/, [u] if the stem vowel is /u, o/. What is crucial for the above discussion is that this vowel carries M tone independent of the tone of the stem vowel. Thus, in the examples we see stems with H, M and L tones. If this were a case of phonetic epenthesis, we would have intermediate representations such as /ttí/ 'screeching', which would have to be broken up by a tonal vowel (not to mention the problem that would arise if we had to consider the /tt/ as a geminate consonant that had to be broken up by epenthesis). In current accounts of reduplication (McCarthy 1981, Marantz 1982), however, this would not be a case of epenthesis. Instead, part or all of a base form is copied, involving part or all of the x-tier and other tiers, as the case may be.

The above discussion is not meant to suggest that the only features that may be epenthesized are on the segmental tier, although this is the normal or most common case. In fact, if epenthesis is reinterpreted as the insertion of features on a single tier, then many rules which we have not termed "epenthetic" turn out to be so. For instance, in Zulu (McLaughren 1984), a L tone is inserted if certain conditions involving "depressor consonants" obtain. This insertion on the tonal tier is essentially an epenthetic process, since the tonal sequence will not otherwise "be pronounceable". Similarly, in Shambaa, where a H autosegment automatically downsteps if preceded by another H autosegment, one might epenthesize a L between every two H's on the tonal tier (but see Odden 1982, who proposes a metrical account of this phenomenon). Or, the Tonga case described by Goldsmith (1982 and elsewhere), could be reanalyzed in the spirit of Meeussen's (1963) original analysis as follows: let each of Meeussen's "determinant" tones be an underlying L, and then insert a free H tone between every two L's. In the framework of underspecified tonality ("incomplete tonification") exemplified in Hyman (1983b), Hyman and Byarushengo (1984), and Pulleyblank (1983), toneless TBU's may receive a tone either by a specified tone insertion (epenthesis) rule sensitive to surrounding tones, or by default tone assignment, e.g. any TBU not having a tone at a certain stage in the derivation receives such and such a tone, typically a L in a two-tone system, a M in a three-tone system, etc.

The view of epenthesis presented in this section allows us to treat certain units as "less than a segment", where this "less" means "not having its own WU". In many cases this is clearly desirable, since less than a segment is being inserted. With time a language may come to treat a historically epenthetic segment as underlying. As an underlying segment it has its own WU which is indistinguishable from WU's of corresponding etymological segments. Thus, weightless epenthesis gives way to weighted segmentality. In a period of transition the conflicting analyses will therefore necessarily be insertion without a WU or an underlying segment with a WU. At no time will there be an analysis requiring insertion *with* a WU, which has been prohibited in this theory of epenthesis.

Chapter 6

Glides

Perhaps the most problematic segment type for all theories of phonology is the class of glides. These segments, including at least [w], [y], [u], and a "gamma-glide", but for some also [h] and [?], have received different interpretations according to the theorist and according to the language in question. Thus, the [+high] glides have been variously referred to as semi-vowels and semi-consonants and the [+glottal] segments, because of their phonological behavior, have sometimes been classified along with the glides, at other times with obstruents. In the Jakobsonian feature framework glides were characterized as [-cons, -voc], thereby accounting for their relationship both to vowels, which are also [-cons], and to consonants, which were viewed also as [-voc]. The feature [voc] has been largely discarded, though there have been recent attempts to reintroduce it or a related version of it. Replacing it in Chomsky and Halle (1968) were the features [syll] and [son]. Glides are [-syll] like (non-syllabic) consonants, and they are [+son] like vowels, nasals and liquids.

In all of the work on syllable structure and the CV tier of the past few years there has, to my knowledge, been no systematic reinterpretation of glides. It has generally been accepted that glides are, in the case of the [+high] segments, vowel features dominated by a C node, whereas the corresponding high vowel has the same features dominated by a V node. The difference, then, is one between [-syll], symbolized by the C, and [+syll], symbolized by the V. This has, however, created situations where gliding or vocalization rules which change vowels into glides or glides into vowels must affect the CV tier. In the x-tier model proposed here, this would not be a problem, because C's and V's are not distinguished from one another in terms of a feature [syll], only in terms of weight. Thus, the question arises as to how [y] and [w], for instance, are to be distinguished from the corresponding vowels [i] and [u].

The position I should like to take here is that the feature [cons] is adequate for distinguishing glides from vowels. Vowels are clearly [-cons]. Glides are *on the surface* [+cons]. My interpretation of this feature, then, is that [+cons] segments are contoids, while [-cons] segments are vocoids, to go back to an old distinction. Thus, instead of saying that a language with strict CVCV structure alternates [-syll] and [+syll] segments, I will say that it alternates [+cons] and [-cons] segments. What makes glides so complex in their variable behavior across languages is that they may either start out as vowels, i.e. as [-cons], or they may start out as consonants, i.e. as [+cons]. In the course of a derivation, as is well known, they may function at one point in the derivation as a vowel, only to function later as a consonant, and so forth. If, however, a vowel does not become [+cons] at the systematic phonetic level, then it is not a glide. I thus interpret the contrast in (116) as follows:

(116) a.   b.

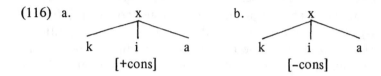

In (116a), where the i is [+cons], we have phonetic [kᵞa]. In (116b), where i is [-cons], we have phonetic [ki̯a], where the symbol ◠ indicates the sequence ia constitutes a single vowel unit. In the CV approach both i and a would be dominated by a single V. In the WU approach the single x in (116b) accounts for the unitary nature of the vowel sequence. The specification of [cons] will determine whether the two segments reporting to the same WU constitute a short vowel sequence, or whether one of the segments is a glide. Since languages make distinctions such as in (116), this appears to be an appropriate way of capturing them.

What is gained by treating all would–be glides, including [h] and [ʔ], as [+cons] is important: these segments will, if followed by a [-cons] segment, undergo the OCR automatically to form a single branching WU. In the following subsections we will see examples of the OCR applying to glides. We might ask if anything is *lost* by treating glides as [+cons]? The [-cons] specification was designed to capture the relationship between glides and vowels. Now if in a language glides start out as underlying vowels, we can maintain the [-cons] specification to refer to both. If, on the other hand, there is a language where glides are [+cons], but where we need to refer to the class of glides and vowels with a single feature, there is a potential difficulty. The prediction that my proposal makes is that no language which treats glides as [+cons] from the very beginning, i.e. from underlying representations on, will need to refer to a single class of glides and vowels.[23] I know of no counterexamples to this claim which, if not correct, should be easily falsified.

6.1. Glides from underlying vowels

In this section I will discuss cases of where surface glides derive from underlying vowels. The most frequent case is the gliding of [+high] vowels when followed by another vowel, e.g. /kia/ becoming [kya]. In CV phonology we would presumably require the V dominating the high vowel to either become a C (if there is reason to treat [ky] as a consonant cluster), or to delete, with the /i/ associating with the preceding C, creating a single consonant segment with a palatal offglide, i.e. [k^y]. In WU phonology, a different statement is required.

Consider the case of French. A well–known rule glides a high vowel followed by another vowel, provided that the high vowel is preceded by at most one consonant:

(117) a. /uɛst/   (ouèst)   → [wɛst]   'west'
      b. /ruɛtə/   (rouette)   → [rwɛt]   'osier band'
      c. /bruɛtə/   (brouette) → [bruɛt]   'wheel-barrow'

In (117a) the vowel /u/ appears without a preceding consonant and glides to become the onset on the following vowel. In (117b), the same vowel, preceded by a single consonant /r/, also becomes a glide. In (117c), however, where the [+high] vowel is preceded by *two* consonants, glide formation is blocked. The derivations for these three forms are given in (118).

(118)

a.
```
x x x x
| | | |
u ɛ s t
```

          GF
```
x x x
/\ | |
u  ɛ s t
```

          MCR
```
    x
  /|\
 u ɛ  s t
```

b.
```
x x x x
| | | |
r u ɛ t
```

          OCR
```
x   x x
/\  | |
r u  ɛ t
```

          GF
```
x     x
/\    |
r u   ɛ t
```

          MCR
```
    x
  /|\
 r u  ɛ t
```

c.
```
x x x x x
| | | | |
b r u ɛ t
```

          OCR
```
x x   x x
| /\  | |
b r u  ɛ t
```

          OAR
```
  x   x x
 /|\  | |
b r u ɛ t
```

          MCR
```
  x     x
 /|\   /\
b r u ɛ  t
```

(UR)

(OCR)

(OAR)

(GF)

(MCR)

The underlying representations are given in the top line of (118). The OCR applies in (118b) and (118c), since we have in both rouette and brouette a

[+cons] segment followed by a [–cons] segment. The OCR does not apply in (118a), however, since the word ouèst begins with a sequence of two [–cons] segments. In the next line of the derivation, a single application of the French onset adjunction rule (OAR) applies in (118c), removing the WU of the initial /b/ and joining it to the following WU. At this point the rule of glide formation (GF) applies in (118a) and (118b). This rule, which we formalize as in (119),

(119)

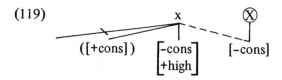

$$([+cons]) \quad \begin{bmatrix} -cons \\ +high \end{bmatrix} \quad [-cons]$$

does not apply in (118c), because it may not be the case that GF creates more than a ternary branching WU.[24] Finally, the surface forms are derived in (118) by an application of the French MCR which applies in each form (twice in (118a)), removing the WU of a [+cons] segment which joins the WU of a preceding [–cons] segment.

A slight complication is found in other cases of glide formation. Thus, consider the process of GF accompanied by compensatory lengthening in Luganda and certain closely related Bantu languages. A sequence of a [+cons] segment followed by a [+high] vowel followed by a (non–identical) vowel will result in a CGVV sequence, i.e. a consonant + glide + geminate vowel. Clements (1982) proposes to handle this development as in (120).

(120)   C   V   V   →   C   V   V   →   C   V   V   [kʸaa]
        | | | ∧ | ∧   ∨
        k   i   a   k   i   a   k   i   a

Starting with a CV tier, Clements disassociates the [+high] vowel from its V and reassociates it with the preceding C. This leaves open its V, which receives a second association from the /a/ to the right. Thus, from /kia/ we obtain [kʸaa]. In my framework the derivation in (121) is proposed.

(121)   x   x   x   →   x   x   →   x   x
        | | | ∧ | ∧⎯⎯⎯⎯⌐
        k   i   a   k   i   a   k   i   a

First the OCR applies creating the two WU's ki-a. Then a rule of GF applies, association the /a/ backwards onto the first x, yielding the correct output.

There is, however, a problem with both Clements' and my account. It happens that in Luganda the compensatory lengthening is observed only if there is a [+cons] segment preceding the glide. Thus, while /tu-a-lab-a/

H H H H

'we saw' is pronounced [twáálàbà] (=[t^{W}áálàbà]), with a geminate [aa], /u-a-lab-a/ 'you sg. saw' is pronounced [wàlábà], i.e. with a short vowel.

H H H

We know that the subject marker /u-/ 'you sg.' (and several other morphemes like it) is [-cons], since it is realized as a vowel when followed by a consonant, e.g. /u-lab-a/ 'you sg. see' is pronounced [òlábà] (with

H

lowering of vowel height in word-initial position). Thus, we must account for the different facts obtained when there is vs. is not a consonant preceding the glided high vowel.

There are at least three possibilities. First, we could assume that there is a special rule deleting the WU of a [-cons] segment which occurs after a word boundary and is followed by another [-cons] WU. This now floating [-cons] segment could then by convention or special rule associate to the WU to the right to create the glide followed by short vowel. As seen in (122),

(122)

$$\left\{ \begin{matrix} [\text{-cons}] \\ \\ \# \end{matrix} \right\} \quad \begin{matrix} \bigotimes \\ | \\ [\text{-cons}] \end{matrix} \quad \begin{matrix} x \\ | \\ [\text{-cons}] \end{matrix}$$

this rule is collapseable with another rule of "vowel truncation" according to which a [-cons] WU is deleted if preceded by a [-cons] segment and followed by another [-cons] WU. Both processes are clearly "post-lexical" and there would be no reason not to express them as a single process.

A second possibility would be to have a readjustment rule preceding the phonology (and hence the OCR) according to which a word-initial [-cons] segment is changed to [+cons] when it is followed by another [-cons] segment. With this readjustment, the OCR would then treat the initial [+high] segment in 'you sg. saw' as a consonant, and we would not get the compensatory lengthening observed in cases of post-consonant gliding.

Both of these approaches treat word-initial /iV/ and /uV/ as exceptional, as does Clements (in press), who literally marks these sequences as such. There is, however, reason to believe that these are not exceptional derivations. A number of vocalic morphemes are involved, and since their exceptionality is predictable from their phonological shape, it seems redundant and undesirable not to provide a phonological solution.

The third solution is inspired from Steriade (1984). In Steriade (1982) the proposal was made that a CV sequence always is always analyzed as tautosyllabic, an observation which, of course, has been incorporated into my OCR. The feature distinguishing C and V is [syll]. Thus, her CV-linking rule essentially says that a [-syll] segment joins a following [+syll] segment in creating a syllable. In Steriade (1984) the following proposals are made to account for the gliding characteristics of high vowels in Rumanian: (a) high vowels are [o syll]; (b) the CV-linking rule applies left-to-right; and (c) [o syll] is interpreted as *either* [+syll] *or* [-syll], whichever interpretation would result in the first application of CV-linking as it scans the input segments from left to right. In other words, in a [-syll] [o syll] sequence, the [o syll] would be treated as a vowel, but in a [o syll] [+syll] sequence, it would be treated as a consonant. (Presumably a [o syll] [o syll] sequence would also come out as a CV.) While this is an unusual interpretation to assign to a zero specification of a feature, it does make the correct prediction also for Luganda: high vowels may surface as either onsets or nuclei (so to speak), according to a left-to-right lining up of the relevant segments with a CV structure. This suggestion captures the intuition that if a high vowel is to be an onset from her CV-linking rule, there should be no compensatory lengthening.

Within the WU approach, we may assume that high vowels are [o cons] and that the OCR has the same left-to-right operation as Steriade proposes - and, crucially, that the zero specification means "interpret as either + or -". Thus, /tua/ and /ua/ would have the underlying specifications in (123).

(123) a.

[+cons]   [o cons]   [-cons]   b.   [o cons]   [-cons]

As seen, in (123a), the [o cons] functions as a [-cons] segment and the OCR removes the WU of the preceding [+cons] segment. (Later the GF rule will associate the [-cons] matrix /a/ to the WU to its left to derive [twaa].) In (123b), on the other hand, the [o cons] functions as [+cons] and its WU is therefore deleted by the OCR, assigning the matrix /u/ to the following WU, as desired. The difference between a language which is like Luganda and a language which treats all glide formation uniformly is potentially attributable to whether the underlying vowels are [-cons] or [o cons]. In any case, *surface* glides must somehow receive the specification [+cons], as I have argued above.

The above alternatives require further study as does the nature of glide segments in general. In particular we would have to explain why it is only the feature [cons] which has this peculiar interpretation of the

zero specification as opposed to other cases of underspecification, where
[o F] would fail to satisfy the conditions for a rule requiring either [+F]
or [-F] (see Kiparsky 1982, Pulleyblank 1983).

6.2. Glides from underlying consonants

In many languages some or all glides are underlyingly consonants, hence
[+cons]. Even these may, apparently, alternate with vowels, as we have
already seen in Berber as in the derivation in (124).

(124) /y + ša/ → [iša] 'he gave'

Penchoen treats the third person singular prefix as a consonant /y/, and it
is clear in at least some cases that it must so be interpreted. Similarly,
in my approach, I would have to consider glides in Cairene Arabic to be
[+cons]. As Broselow (1976) has pointed out, words such as abyad
'white' must be syllabified as ab.yad, not as *a.byad. That is, there can
be no onset clusters and glides count as a consonant for this purpose.
This is not surprising, given McCarthy's (1981) separation of lexical vs.
grammatical morphemes onto different tiers. Lexical roots consist only
of consonants, e.g. /ktb/ 'write', which McCarthy has associate onto C
slots on a CV skeleton or template. This template could, however, be seen
as consisting of x's each of which is prespecified as either [+cons] or
[-cons], i.e. the "top" feature of the respective segmental matrices is
already specified. Thus, when a root such as /ysr/ 'play with a dreydl'
is mapped onto the template, it assumes [+cons] slots. On the other
hand, when the vowels /uai/ 'perfective passive' are mapped, they assume
[-cons] slots. Thus, when it comes to creating WU's and syllables in
Arabic, glides will be [+cons] and vowels will be [-cons], as desired.

In (13) above it was stated that there cannot be an opposition between
a syllabic vs. non-syllabic marginal consonant, where in each case the consonant has a WU of its own. This followed from the assertion that having
a WU is tantamount to being syllabic, i.e. each WU defines a [+syllabic]
unit, though the "peak" or carrier of the syllabicity will depend on a
sonority scale, as has been proposed for syllable construction itself. The
question which correspondingly can be raised for glides is whether a
language may oppose representations such as in (125).

(125) a.   x   x   b.   x   x

            /\ | /\ |

           t   a   i   t   a   y

The example in (125a) has a vowel sequence, where the second vowel which is [+high] is intended to be [+syll], parallel to the syllabic nasal in (13a). The example in (125b), on the other hand, has a glide, presumably [+cons] so that it can be distinct from the high vowel in (125a), with its own WU. Were this glide not to have a WU, i.e. were the three segments in (125b) to report to a single WU, there would be no question but that an opposition with (125a) is possible. The discussion of this and the preceding section would predict that (125a,b) may be contrastive, since the /i/ may be [−cons] and the /y/ [+cons]. Since there has been no reason to suppose that a weighted nasal or liquid may be [−cons], the two representations in (13a) may not contrast, as we have said. Perhaps the complex facts of Hausa plural formation discussed by Newman (1972) and Newman and Salim (1981), among others, may justify representations such as the above. Without going into all of the detail that has been the subject of much debate among Hausaists (see also Schuh 1972, Leben 1974, 1977a,b), consider the following plural patterns exemplified in (126).

(126) a. máísóó / máísààyéé   'unworked farm/s'
           zóómóó / zóómààyéé   'hare/s'
       b. káymíí / káyààméé   'spur/s'
           gúlbíí / gúlààbéé   'stream/s'

At stake here is whether orthographic ai should be analyzed as in (125a) or (125b) in Hausa. In (126a) we see that 'unworked farms' follows the plural pattern of 'hares', suggesting that the ai is to be represented as a sequence of vowels, as in (125a). In (126b), on the other hand, 'spurs' follows the plural pattern of 'streams', suggesting that the ai is to be represented as a vowel + glide sequence. Newman and Salim show that most of the arguments support the second segment as a "true vocalic diphthong". This category is somewhat mute in our framework, since the /y/ or /w/ element of a diphthong can be either [+cons] or [−cons] here, which is of course the issue at stake in these Hausa forms. Since much of the point of the discussion between Newman, Schuh and Leben concerns the variability of such plural forms and others, perhaps Hausa speakers are struggling at the moment to determine which of two possible representations, (125a) or (125b), should be given to each diphthong - with disagreement, inconsistency, dialect variation etc. Since in either case the glide must be tone-bearing, we know that we are dealing with two WU's and not a single WU dominating two segmental matrices. It is, thus, possible to have the opposition in (125a,b) within the same language.

Given that glides may be either [+cons] or [−cons], and given that they may have weight or not, what about cases of epenthetic glides? Are they [+cons] or [−cons]? It would make great sense if epenthetic glides having their own feature matrix always were [+cons]. In Berber, for instance, vowel sequences are usually interrupted by a [y]:

(127) a. /ddu/ 'go' + /at/ 'imper.m.pl.' → [dduyaθ]
      b. /bla/ 'without' + /udi/ 'butter' → [βlayuði]

In a framework having a feature syllabic, the motivation behind such cases of glide insertion would be to place a [-syll] segment between two [+syll] segments. In WU phonology, however, there is no feature [syll] and no CV tier (and even no syllables in some languages, perhaps Berber). We must suppose, then, that the motivation behind y-epenthesis in Berber is to break the hiatus, i.e. to place a [+cons] segment between two [-cons] segments. Of course, we could also view the motivation as the desire to maximize branching WU's, i.e. WU's with an onset. I know of no argument, however, for viewing epenthetic glides as initially being [-cons]. As I have suggested, *all* glides are [+cons] on the surface, so it is merely a question as to *when* a glide will receive its [+cons] specification. Since there appears to be no reason to do it later, an epenthetic glide with its own feature matrix will be introduced with a [+cons] specification.

Chapter 7

Recapitulation and Discussion

In the preceding sections I have presented an alternative view to the question of hierarchical structure in phonology. Rather than segments being constructed directly into syllables, there is a universal weight tier of "beats", with each WU or x representing potential syllabicity. Syllables were said to be a language-particular construct. Though it has appeared from the first work in phonology that syllables are universal, the results presented in this study suggest that a new look should be taken at many of the cases where the syllable was believed to have been at work. I assume especially in the case of languages exhibiting a contrast between heavy and light syllables that the syllable is a necessary level of prosodic representation.

To recapitulate the major points of the preceding sections, the following has been suggested, first for underlying representations:

(a) The universal anchor tier or core is a weight tier, where each WU (or x) stands for a potential beat (or mark of syllabicity).

(b) The universal segmental tier consists of feature matrices headed by the feature [cons] which, as we have seen, plays a special role in this theory (cf. also section 9).

(c) There may, in addition, be language specific autosegmental tiers, especially in languages with tone, vowel harmony, nasal prosodies and the like.

Concerning the kinds of rules needed, the following has been said, first concerning the WU's:

(a) There is a universal onset creation rule (OCR) which automatically removes the WU of a [+cons] segment when it is followed by a WU dominating a [-cons] segment. The [+cons] feature matrix simultaneously associates onto the [-cons] WU to its right.

(b) There may be language-specific onset adjunction rules (OAR's), which assign additional [+cons] segments to the WU to the right, also removing their own WU. There appears to be evidence that at least in some cases these OAR's need to precede the margin construction.

(c) There are language specific margin creation rules (MCR's) which add a [+cons] segment to a preceding [-cons] WU, removing its own WU.

(d) There may be language-specific margin adjunction rules (MAR's), which assign additional [+cons] segments to the WU to the left, also removing their own WU.

(e) There are language specific syllable formation rules which may build syllables out of the WU's in a given language.

(f) Finally, a language may have a late rule adding so-called appendix or extrasyllabic [+cons] segments to the preceding syllable. It may be that many of these processes are simply late applications of an additional MAR, though the relationship between these two operations is a subject requiring further study in this (and other) frameworks.

The additional rules that are needed in this theory are the following:

(a) Rules that map autosegments onto WU's, e.g. autosegmental features of tone, nasality, vowel harmony, etc.

(b) Rules that change features, insert segments, and delete segments, i.e. the "P-rules" in linear phonology.

Let us consider the implications of each of these components of the WU theory.

(a) The tripartite distinction between a core (here, of WU's), a set of autosegmental tiers, and a segmental tier is non-controversial except for our insistence on WU's rather than on C's and V's or X's/T's standing for [+seg]. In our theory the feature matrices are the "segments". The x's are the "beats" and are related to segments directly only in underlying representations, where each segment can be accompanied by one, two or zero WU's. Apparently there is never any need for a single feature matrix to be associated to three WU's; in section 9 I shall propose that a WU may at most be ternary in its branching characteristics. It may also, of course, have a single or double segmental association, or it may have no segmental association at all in cases where a WU exists without any corresponding features on the segmental tier. Of the three kinds of tiers (the weight tier, the segmental tier and any autosegmental tiers), only the first two are universal.

(b) Once we accept the concept of WU's it is clear that there will be rules deleting many of the potential beats that are present in underlying forms. The universal OCR is one such rule that exists in all languages. Languages which create "closed WU's" by adding a [+cons] segment to a CV WU will require a MCR, which, since it is language-specific, may have stipulations on it, e.g. only [-son] consonants or only consonants without a tonal association may undergo it, etc. It should be clear that these language specific rules deleting WU's may apply interspersed among other rules, e.g. we may first map the tonal tier onto the WU's surviving the OCR, and only afterwards delete the WU of any [+cons] to become a margin of a WU. Similarly, in languages which allow more than one consonant to serve as onset of a WU or as margin of a WU, the [+cons] adjunction rules may be interspersed in such a way that their x may count at an earlier stage of the derivation, but not at a later stage. The reverse should not be possible. As a case in point, Donca Steriade (personal communication) has pointed out the Classical Greek case where it is necessary to refer to heavy vs. light syllables at an early stage in the phonology (where heavy = CVV or CVC, and light = CV) in the determining of the placement of accent, but that only vowels are tone-bearing in this language. What this means is that for the purposes of accent placement we have the syllable representations in (128), but for the purpose of tone mapping we have the syllable representations in (129).

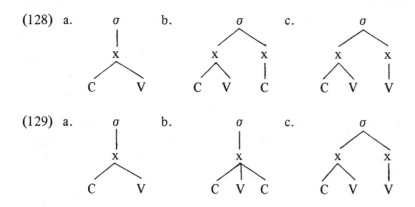

In (128) only the OCR has applied and both CVC and CVV are heavy syllables, since (128b) and (128c) have syllables consisting of two WU's. (In the above examples, C stands for [+cons] and V stands for [-cons], contrary to common practice. I shall follow this practice from here on out.) These are the structures that are relevant for accent placement in Classical Greek. The structures in (129) differ only in that the CVC sequence, which counted as two WU's for the placement of accent, counts as only *one* WU for the mapping of tone. What has happened in going from (128b) to (129b), then, is that a margin creation rule has applied subsequent to accent placement, i.e. the drawing of metrical trees or grids, but prior to the mapping of the H tone. In an early discussion in this paper it was suggested that the same "projections" are needed for both accent and tone. We can now refine this statement as follows: it should be possible to acquire different projections for these or other phonological mapping, but these different projections should always have the property of earlier projections referring to more WU information than later projections. Of course, by projection in this system I mean "reference to the WU's", since there are no projections per se. It should be highly unlikely, if this theory is correct, to find a language which must at an early stage in the derivation refer to CV/CVC vs. CVV syllables, but in a later stage in the derivation refer to CV vs. CVC/CVV syllables. Perhaps once the syllable weight issue is reinterpreted in terms of WU's, a version of the elsewhere condition (Kiparsky 1973) may make the same prediction, since the earlier "projection" includes the later "projection", though there is no need to invoke this principle here when the independently required MCR makes exactly the same prediction.

Two questions which arise are the following: (i) Are there any phonological rules that apply before the OCR? (ii) Are there any rules that *add* WU's?

Concerning the first question, the strongest position we could possibly take – and the one I would like to assume, at least tentatively, is that *no* phonological rule may apply before the OCR. There seem to be two kinds of complications that arise out of this position. The first involves cases where the onset consonant has an opaque autosegmental association; the second involves cases where a [+cons] segment is epenthesized between the would-be onset and the following vowel. Concerning the first, we shall see examples involving nasality and vowel harmony in section 8, so I will not discuss this problem in depth here. We can note, however, that if an opaquely associated segment loses its WU through the OCR (or otherwise) we have the various possible consequences in (130).

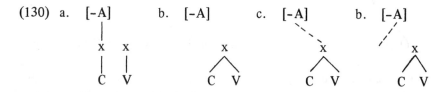

(130) a. [-A]   b. [-A]   c. [-A]   b. [-A]

In (130a) the hypothetical input is provided, where [-A] is opaquely associated with the [+cons] WU. When the OCR applies we obtain (118b), where the [-A] autosegment is no longer associated, since its WU has been deleted. If (130b) remains as the output, a [+A] coming from the left would be able to associate onto the remaining WU, since no lines would cross. In order to prevent this, one of two things might happen. In (130c), the [-A] had reassociated with the remaining WU. This is similar to one of the proposals concerning the floating L of the Kpelle form in (63d). On the other hand, in (130d), the [-A] autosegment is reassociated to an x to the left (not shown), thereby requiring as a consequence of the OCR that the preceding WU have the opaque value. This may not be as odd as it seems. Consider, for example, the case of i-umlaut in Takelma, discussed by Howard (1972). In this language a sequence of /a/'s will become [i] if followed by [i], and if only [+voice] consonants intervene. Howard expresses this as a right-to-left directional rule, though

this needn't concern us here. What we propose is that there be an autosegment [+HIGH], but that [-voice] consonants are opaquely specified
[-HIGH].[25] Now, when the opaquely specified consonant loses its x as
the result of the OCR, the [-HIGH] specification is assigned to the preceding x which, if a vowel, is where the specification needs to go in the
first place. It is hard to find an example where (130d) *must* be the interpretation given to the flotated autosegment, but since its reassociation
will have to be a language specific property, this possibility is expected to
be borne out. The question thus becomes one of whether disassociating
opaque autosegments by the OCR creates any problems for languages
with this phenomenon.

The second potential problem for requiring the OCR to be the first
rule of the phonology concerns cases where the surface onset of a WU
is an epenthetic [+cons] segment. One such case could be made for the
so-called aspirated consonants in various Bamileke dialects. As I showed
in Hyman (1972b, 1976), these dialects exhibit a rule aspirating consonants before an underlying high vowel. In some dialects most consonants
are affected (e.g. Dschang); in others, it may be only the obstruents. The
result is that the underlying forms /à-túɨ/ tree' and /Ǹ-búɨ/ 'dog' are
pronounced [àthɨ́ɨ] and [m̀'bhɨ́ɨ] in the Bafou variety of Dschang dialect.
The same "insertion" of an h is observed before /i/ and /u/, although
certain dialects have modified these vowels and/or the consonants, e.g.
th may become t[s], etc. (see Hyman 1976 for discussion). What is critical
in this phenomenon is that the predictable "aspiration" or "aspiration
plus frication" has impressed everyone as a "full segment", rather than a
feature change as in the case of English aspiration. The reason for this,
I believe, is that the h is the onset grouping with the following vowel,
whereas the underlying consonant is assigned to the *preceding* WU. One
way to do this would be to insert the h prior to the OCR, as in (131).

(131)
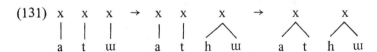

First the epenthetic [h] is inserted (without a weight unit, as per the
generalization claimed in section 5.5), forming the onset onto the vowel
/ɯ/. Now, most languages would go on to adjoin the /t/ to the following
WU, deleting its WU, in which case we would derive à-t[h]ɨ́ɨ. However,
this is exactly what all Bamileke scholars have balked at. The [h] appears
to be separated from the preceding consonant. This is represented in the
last stage of the derivation in (131), where the /t/ is assigned to the *preceding* WU, losing its own WU. In cases where there is no preceding WU
such as a vowel or syllabic nasal, the impression is that the initial con-

sonant is exploded *on its own beat* followed by a [hV] beat. That is, these initial consonants preceding the epenthetic [h] are not part of the following WU - they constitute their own WU. One side benefit of this analysis is that the word 'dog' in Dschang, which would consist of the WU's m̀b-'hɯ́ɯ́ (where ' is a tonal downstep marker), no longer seems an anomaly: had it been divided as m̀-'bhɯ́ɯ́, we would have a voiced aspirate, i.e. a WU starting with a [+voice] onset, becoming [−voice], and then again [+voice], something which may not even be attested in languages. Ladefoged (1971) and elsewhere has argued that what phonologists call voiced aspirates are really breathy voice consonants. Dschang clearly has the sequencing of voicing as indicated, but because the /b/ is not part of the following onset, but rather belongs to the preceding WU, we can maintain Ladefoged's position, and at the same time recognize Dschang [bh] sequences for what they are.

There are quite a number of related phenomena which might be viewed in this same way. For example, in Shona, underlying /Np, Nt, Nk/ are realized as [mɦ, nɦ, ɦ] (Guthrie 1971:62). The normal assumption is that the voiceless stops became aspirated after nasals and then lost their place of articulation. (The velar nasal subsequently drops.) In the same language /Cw/ sequences have a complex realization, e.g. /sw/ is realized [sxw], /rw/ is realized [rɣw] etc. Now, if we assume that the extra segment, whether [ɦ], [x] or [ɣ] forms the onset of the following vowel, we can, in assigning the preceding consonant to the preceding WU, account in a unified way for certain of these sequential complications and sequential simplifications: the WU nt becomes n, etc. In other words, it may not be accidental that Shona introduces both aspiration in the way it does as well as obstruentization of [w].

How would this all be accomplished if we required that the OCR be universally applied as the first phonological rule? We would then have the derivation of 'tree' in Dschang as in (132):

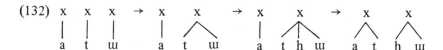

(132) x   x   x   →   x   x   →   x   x   →   x   x

a   t   ɯ   a   t   ɯ   a   t   h   ɯ   a   t   h   ɯ

We start with the same three WU's as in (131). The first rule is the OCR, which removes the WU of the /t/ sending it to the WU to the right. At this point we epenthesize the [h] to the second WU in between the [t] and the [ɯ]. The final step is the reassignment of the [t] from the onset of the second WU to the margin of the preceding WU. Thus, the real disadvantage of this analysis is that it requires three rules rather than two. It also requires a special rule we have not seen much evidence for, namely one which takes from an onset and creates a preceding margin. In cases

I am familiar with, e.g. Arabic syllabification of word-initial CC clusters, I would want to claim that the first C in the cluster did not go through an onset stage, but rather maintains its WU, creating a (heavy) syllable with a preceding vowel across a word boundary (see Broselow 1976). We did, however, see something roughly similar to the last step of (132) in our discussion of the syllabic liquid in Idoma. In this language, as seen in (68b), the onset liquid acquires a *second* association onto the preceding WU. Whether this should be viewed as creating a margin on the first WU is obviously not important, since the only issue is that the WU requires sufficient sonority in order to realize its tone. I will assume, then, that we can maintain the OCR as the first rule of the phonology until further evidence against it is presented. There are, of course, what I have termed "readjustment rules" affecting WU's which apply prior to the OCR, e.g. affecting vowels which become glides, but these are, strictly speaking, not rules of the phonology.

The second question which was raised is whether there are any rules *adding* WU's. The alternative is that there may only be rules deleting WU's, instances of which we have seen aplenty. The segment addition rules we have discussed all involve epenthesis, and it has been hypothesized that epenthetic segments are never inserted with a WU of their own. Thus, if this generalization holds, epenthesis is not an argument for a WU addition process.

Rules that add WU's might be ones which lengthen vowels or consonants in certain positions. Some of these are clearly syllable-related and, as will be seen, should not involve the addition of a WU. Others such as in Estonian (Prince 1980) may be foot-related and also do not involve the addition of a WU. The extra lengths which are added by such processes rarely seem to be counted by the phonological rules of stress placement, for instance. Thus, consider two hypothetical languages. The first, Language A, was described in (Hyman 1977:49) with the following derivations:

(133) a.　/papaba/　→　papa:ba　→　papá:ba
　　　　　/papapa/　　　　　　　→　pápapa

This language has a rule lengthening vowels before voiced consonants, something which is widely attested in languages (see Chen 1970, Lehiste 1970). The stress rule is stated as follows: stress the penultimate syllable if it has a long vowel, otherwise stress the antepenultimate syllable. (133a) shows that the length deriving from the following [+voice] consonant feeds into the first clause of the stress assignment rule. However, no such language has ever been described. In fact, the generalization which I proposed in Hyman (1973b) is that tone may be sensitive to consonant types while stress may not be (but cf. below). If (133) were possible as a language, the rule could equally be stated as "stress the penultimate syllable if the final syllable begins with a voiced consonant, otherwise stress the penultimate syllable", with the vowel lengthening in the penultimate syllable being irrelevant. It therefore must not be the case that we allow such lengthening to involve the addition of a WU, or else we must stipulate that stress rules must always precede this WU–addition rule. A different solution will be proposed in a moment.

Consider a second language, Language B, which has the derivations in (134).

(134)   a.   /papapap/   →   pa:pa:pap   →   pa:pá:pap
      b.   /papappap/   →   pa:pappap   →   pá:pappap

This language has a rule that lengthens vowels in open syllable and a stress rule which stresses the last long vowel in a word. As seen in the examples, this results in the penultimate syllable being stressed in (134a), but in the antepenultimate syllable being stressed in (134b). What is significant and troublesome in this hypothetical language is that a closed syllable is being passed over in (134a) and *two* closed syllables are being passed over in (134b), in order for a CV syllable to receive stress. In other words, one could state the stress rule as follows: "stress the last CV syllable of the word". In this formulation one sees what is wrong with Language B. In Language B a CV syllable would thus count as heavy, while a CVC syllable would count as light. Vowel lengthening would be irrelevant to this statement of the stress rule. And yet, this kind of situation is never found. Thus, I conclude again, that this vowel lengthening process should not involve the addition of another WU, or else we would have no non–ad hoc way of stopping a stress rule from referring to the added WU.

It is sometimes pointed out that vowels are lengthened in open syllable or other contexts within a given language, but that the result is not equal to a geminate or underlying long vowel. As an example, let us turn to the other common lengthening rule motivated by syllables and stress: the one which lengthens consonants in a syllable with a given relationship to the placement of stress. An example comes from Island Carib, which lengthens the consonants /b, f, m, t, d, s, n, r, l, g/ "in post–stress syllables" (Taylor 1954:234). The result, however, is not equivalent to a geminate consonant, as Taylor's following examples demonstrate:

(135)   a.   /mátadi + ti/   →   [mátatti]   'he doesn't/cannot drink'
      b.   /máta + ti/   →   [mátat:i]   'he is bloodless/doesn't bleed'

Taylor states explicitly that the lengthened [t:] in (135b) is not as long as the geminate [tt] in (135a). And yet it *is* lengthened.

The solution is to propose a representation of these kinds of lengthening processes without having to add more WU's. I propose that open-syllable lengthening be represented as in (136a), and that consonant lengthening such as the one illustrated in (135b) be represented as in (136b).

(136) a.

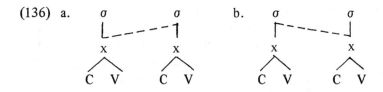

In (136a) we associate the first x to the second syllable as a late rule indicating that it gets more duration (though not more weight). The extra duration will automatically be realized on the latter part of the initial WU, i.e. on the vowel. In (136b) we have intervocalic consonant lengthening (probably induced by stress considerations), which I have indicated as the first syllable acquiring an additional association from the second syllable. This will result in greater duration given to the initial part of the second syllable, i.e. the consonant. Now representations such as in (136) will not create heavy syllables if we require either that such cases of "syllable linking" be disallowed as a phonological process, i.e. it takes place after the "core phonology", or that an x which belongs to two syllables does not contribute weight to both. The alternative would seem to be associating the lengthened vowel or consonant directly to the syllable node. Of course, the claim is made in (136) that such lengthening rules are syllable-sensitive, something which may need further attention. Nothing is said in (136a) about vowel lengthening before pause, which also must be looked at in light of the fact that some languages lengthen, while other languages shorten vowels in this position. Finally, the reason why we don't simply associate the [t] of (135b) with both x's is that this will be the representation of the true geminate (unless the difference can be maintained as one [+cons] matrix in (135b) but two in (135a), as recognized by Schein (1981) and Kenstowicz (1982) for Tigrinya, for instance). As can be seen, this is an area in need of further investigation before a definitive stand can be taken.

Returning to the issues raised at the beginning of this subsection, a few words need to be said about syllable formation rules and segmental rules. Some languages go on to construct syllables, others do not. It is my claim that many of the syllable analyses given in the recent literature need not involve the syllable and that we are in need of a theory that will tell us exactly when and where syllables are constructed as a distinct level in the prosodic hierarchy. I would like to discuss one argument for the syllable here and show how the structure of the syllable I have proposed, with x's being its immediate constituents, explains one interesting constraint on stress rules.

In the first section of this paper we discussed the well-known phenomenon of syllable weight. Stress assignment may be sensitive to whether a syllable branches or not. Or, equivalently, to whether a syllable consists of one x (=light) or more than one (at most two?) x's (=heavy). One of the points I made in Hyman (1973b), picked up also by E. Pike (1974), is that tone may be sensitive to consonant types (e.g. voiced vs. voiceless), but stress never is (cf. the discussion surrounding the hypothetical Language A in (133)). No explanation was given for this fact, i.e. the fact that no language has a rule stressing the penultimate syllable unless it begins with a voiced consonant, in which case one stresses the antepenultimate syllable, etc. It was merely asserted that tone languages may have rules sensitive to the voicing parameter in consonants, while stress languages may not.

I believe that the framework developed here can provide a principled, formal explanation for this observation. Stress is normally (universally?) a property of *syllables*, while tone is normally (universally?) a property of WU's. Assuming that these are, at the very least, the *unmarked* P-bearing units for stress vs. tone, the explanation is now in sight: in assigning a feature to a P-bearing unit, the rule is allowed to look only *one level down*. In other words, any rule assigning features to syllables will only be able to look at the units dominated by the syllable node, i.e. the x's in my framework, and *not* at the units dominated in turn by the x's. Any rule assigning features to x's, on the other hand, will be allowed to look one level down at what the x's dominate, i.e. the segmental features, such as [voice], [son], etc. That the stress vs. tone dichotomy is not sufficient is seen from the fact that so-called pitch- or tonal accent languages may be sensitive to the voicing parameter, e.g. Digo (Kisseberth 1984). The reason for this is that in pitch accent languages it is the WU that receives the accent, normally in the form of a H tone placement rule, as in Japanese dialects (McCawley 1977, Haraguchi 1977), Somali (Hyman 1980), Lithuanian (Kenstowicz 1970), Creek (Haas 1977), etc. In the standard formulation of the syllable, built as it is from a CV tier, this generalization cannot be captured. This, then, consitutes more evidence for the framework being developed here.[27]

A further issue requiring discussion is the structure of segmental matrices and the rules affecting them. I shall make the following assumptions, based in part on Clements' work and on McCarthy's insightful treatment of morphological tiers and their mapping:

(a) There is a distinct segmental matrix of features. That is, in most or all languages with only concatenative morphology, one can isolate a tier that has special status and does not have autosegmental properties.

(b) The role of the autosegmental tiers is to fill in blanks within the segmental matrices. Thus, we will have lots of archisegments, i.e. incompletely specified segments, in languages with autosegmental tiers. In the Arabic case described by McCarthy (1979, 1981), we have the *reverse* of what we normally expect. Instead of having the segmental matrices mostly filled in, with a few blanks, we have the segmental matrices only specified for [cons], with all of the remaining features being specified by the autosegmental tiers, each representing a morpheme. Thus, I assume that McCarthy's templates consist of WU's with prespecified values of the feature [cons], rather than prespecified values of the feature [syll] via the use of a CV tier.

(c) Since the function of autosegmental mapping rules is to fill in blanks it should be clear that autosegmental features do not override segmentally specified ones. The only way to change a feature in a segmental matrix is by a segmental P-rule.[28]

(d) Since autosegments fill in blanks, but since there is no override of features in the segmental matrices, it follows that the blanks may not be filled in by the autosegmental associations except at certain critical points in the phonology. This is especially so because the autosegmental associations may change by rule within a derivation. If an association were to result in the immediate feature specification within the segmental matrix, there would be no way for a new association to override this specification, as it must.

(e) The first feature specification point is achieved prior to the phonological rules. This is where Clements' (1981) opaque and neutral segments are identified: an opaque segment is one which has an autosegmental feature associated with it lexically; a neutral segment is one whose segmental feature is specified, but without a corresponding autosegmental association. The crucial difference between the two is that the first may block an other autosegment from spreading through it, while the latter may not. Thus, the neutral vowels of Hungarian (see Vago 1980 and others) would be considered "neutral" in Clements' sense, since although they themselves are specified as [-back], they permit a [+BACK] autosegment to associate through them. On the other hand, Clements' and Sezer's (1983) analysis of Turkish vowel and consonant harmony is full of cases of opaque associations on consonants which stop an autosegment from affecting subsequent segments. A question which arises is whether opaque segments necessarily have their segmental feature specified at that point. I believe they do. This is especially needed in cases where a segment is opaquely specified for a non-intersecting, or potentially a conflicting, autosegmental feature, e.g. a case where a vowel is [-back] but carries the opaque autosegmental association of [+BACK]. I will therefore assume that every opaque association implies the specification of the corresponding feature whithin the segmental matrix. This makes the prediction that opaque associations not only have their blocking effect, but also are not overriden by changes in autosegmental associations. In other words, the important property of opaque associations is that they are immutable. This may be somewhat too strong a statement, though it seems to be accurate in so many cases that a closer look might reveal some reasonable steps we might take to preserve it.

As part of the "readjustment rules" that immediately precede the phonological rules I would suggest other kinds of prespecifications and preassociations as have been studied by McCarthy and by Lieber (1983, 1984). Both have been concerned with templates that have certain grammatical morphemes encoded in them prior to the insertion (autosegmental association) of lexical roots. In McCarthy's study of Arabic, the association procedure consisted of first spelling out the grammatical morphemes, e.g. the /t/ that crops up in some of the binyanim, and only thereafter spelling out the lexical roots, e.g. /ktb/. I don't believe he took a stand on whether the vowels had to be associated prior to the consonants of a lexical root. If we tried to generalize on the case of the /t/ and other [+cons] associations which might interact with the association of the [+cons] lexical stems, we could say that the templates come with the grammatical consonants *and* vowels preassociated. This would allow the vowels to still be associated by the one-to-one mapping process that works in many of the cases (in all cases except where the final vowel is /i/, apparently), but this process would take place prior to the "real phonology", so to speak. In other words, the association of grammatical morphemes would be *opaque*, including the metathesis rule changing tC to Ct in certain forms.

Chapter 8

The Mapping of Autosegments

The above summarizes the basic properties of the model short of one issue: the mapping of autosegmental features. The basic principle in this mapping is the following: autosegments are mapped onto available WU's, provided that each WU dominates at least one segment (feature matrix) having a blank for the corresponding feature. This generalizes, I believe, on what McCarthy intended for Arabic: in his association of lexical roots, he skips over C slots which already have an association with a (grammatical) consonant. Thus, the mapping process is allowed to search all of the possible autosegmental associations for a given slot to see if there is any [+cons] segment already associated to the C slot in question. My proposal differs only slightly – and the difference is mostly attributable to my adoption of WU's: when an autosegment is to be associated, it checks to see if there is *any* available segment dominated by the WU which can receive its specification. If there is, the WU is taken into account and the autosegment is associated with it. If there is no segment dominated by this WU which is blank with respect to the feature of the autosegment, the WU is skipped over, exactly as in McCarthy's treatment of non-concatenative morphology in Arabic.

It is relatively straightforward to see how this procedure might lead to the avoidance of projections in phonology. If tones go only to vowels, then consonants may be prespecified with tonal features (perhaps stiff/ slack vocal cords, etc., though this requires further investigation). Thus, even if a non-onset consonant maintains its WU at the time of tone association, it will be skipped over if it has a tonal feature specified in its feature matrix. On the other hand, if it is blank with respect to tone in its feature matrix, it will be counted for the purpose of tone association.

In the follwing sections I illustrate the mapping procedures for Gokana, first for nasality, then briefly for tone and vowel harmony.

8.1. The mapping of nasality in Gokana

The suprasegmental nature of nasality in Gokana was accounted for in Hyman (1982b), though what I shall say here supercedes the analysis presented in the earlier paper. The basic facts about the distribution of nasality can be summarized as follows:

(a) A foot has one of three possible nasal characteristics: it may have all oral segments, as in (137a), all nasal segments, as in (137b), or an initial oral consonant followed by all nasal segments, as in (137c).

(137) a. tɔ   'house'   piob   'tsetse fly'
          vái   'bed'   kigi   'axe'
          zib   'thief'   fɔ́ɔ́rɔ́   'wind'
      b. nū   'thing'   mɛ́nɛ̃̀   'chief'
          náã̀   'gun'   nãānà̀   'snake'
          nɔ̃m   'animal'
      c. bã̀   'pot'   bĩɔ̃m   'fingernail'
          bĩɔ̃   'nose'   fĩnĩ   'monkey'
          dɛ̀m   'tongue'   kúũnĩ́   'cooking stone'

The above words are nouns, constituting single feet, but the same properties hold for verb feet, which consist, as we have seen, of a verb root and a possible grade, derivational and inflectional suffix. No other combinations of nasality are possible within a foot. Thus, we cannot start a foot nasally and end it orally, nor can the first CV of the foot be nasal if the second CV is oral or vice-versa. It follows, then, that if the second consonant of a foot is nasal, both preceding and following vowels will also be nasal (but cf. the -mā suffix in (53) above and (143) below).

(b) If the initial consonant is [v], [l] or [z], then all successive segments must be oral, as seen in (138).

(138) a. va   'wife'   b. zob   'dance'
          lí   'root'   zárí   'buy'
          zɔ̀   'pain'   zaari   'scatter'

(c) Finally, recall from the display of Gokana segments in (15) that the vowels [e] and [o] do not occur nasalized.

As seen first for the intransitive suffix /-a/ in (139) and then for the two transitive suffixes /-CÈ/ in (140), verb suffixes alternate in nasality depending on the nasality of the verb root.

(139) a. aè kʸɔ̃   'he spoiled (it)'   aé kʸɔ̀à   'it spoiled'
          aè ʔ ìg   'he twisted (it)'   aè ʔ ìgà   'it twisted'
      b. aè gɔ̃̀   'he spoiled (it)'   aè gɔ̃ã̀   'he hid (himself)'
          aè mɔ̃n   'he saw (it)'   baè mɔ̃̀nã̀   'they saw (each
                                                             other)'

(140) a. aè ʔ ii   'it sank'   aè ʔ iírè̠   'he sank (it)'
          aè pɪ̄ɪ̄   'he became quiet'   aè pɪ̄ɪ̄nɛ̀   'he quieted (s.o.)'
      b. aè gʸɔɔ   'it became wet'   aè gʸɔ̀ɔ̀vɛ̀   'he wet (it)'
          aè kāā   'it dried'   aè kāāmɛ̀̀   'he dried (it)'

In (139) the intransitive suffix is [a] after an oral root and [ā] after
a nasal root. In (140a) we observe a transitive suffix taking the shape
[re] after an oral root, but [nɛ] after a nasal root; and in (140b) we
observe another transitive suffix taking the shape [vɛ] after an oral
root and [mɛ] after a nasal root. The vowel of the oral transitive suffixes is either [e] or [ɛ], depending on vowel harmony (see below).
The [r] in (140a) and the [v] in (140b) are the intervocalic realizations
of the archiphonemes /D/ and /B/ in an oral context, as we shall see below.

In order to account for nasality in Gokana, it is necessary to distingish
between "root" and "non-root" morphemes. Root morphemes include
all morphemes which are not affixes in the *lexical* phonology. That is,
they include lexical morphemes such as noun and verb stems, but also
pronominal stems which may, post-lexically, become cliticized to a preceding noun or verb form. What I would like to propose is, first, that
there is only a [+NAS] autosegment in underlying representations, i.e.
there is no [-NAS] autosegment, and, second, that only roots, as defined above, may have a [+NAS] specification. (We will see that the
-mā suffix is the one exception in the language.) Thus, the root morphemes in (137b) and (137c) will have a [+NAS] autosegment, while
those in (137a) will lack this autosegment, as will those in (138). The
non-root suffixes illustrated in the second column of (139) and (140)
will also lack a nasal specification and will, when suffixed to a [+NAS]
root morpheme, acquire their nasality by the rightward spreading of this
feature. A default spelling rule will account for the unmarked [-nasal]
specification of all segments which do not acquire a [+nasal] specification via the rightward spreading of the [+NAS] autosegment.

The question arises as to how we can account for the "mixed forms"
in (137c), which have an oral initial consonant followed by one or more
nasal segments. As indicated above, this oral segment may be any except
[l], [v] or [z], which require that all subsequent segments be oral. The
initial nasal consonants in the language are [m, ɱ, n, ɲ], where [ɱ] represents a labiodental nasal, orthographically nw, as in nwín [ɱín] 'child'.
The velar nasal [ŋ] does not appear initially in words. It is clear that we
have at least a partial complementary distribution, since the above three
oral consonants do not occur before nasal segments and the above four nasal consonants do not appear before oral segments. One might then represent
the labiodental, alveolar and palatal nasals respectively as /v̄/, / l̄/ and /z̄/.
But what about the bilabial nasal?

I would like to suggest that the above four nasals are realizations of the archisegments /B/, /V/, /D/ and /Z/ when these are associated with a [+NAS] autosegment. Recall at this time the facts about the second consonant of a foot seen earlier in (28) and (29). There it was seen that the second consonant of a foot may be [b], [l] or [g] in an oral foot, or [m], [n] or [ŋ] in a nasal foot. I therefore propose to treat these also as archisegments, i.e. as /B/, /D/ and /G/. The last will never appear as the initial consonant in a foot, since no foot begins with a velar nasal. On the other hand, /B/ will have to contrast in initial position because of triplets such as in (141).

(141) a. /bá/   →   [bá]   'arm'
        b. /bá̰/   →   [bá̰]   'pot'
        c. /Bá̰/   →   [má̰]   'breast'

In order to prevent the [+NAS] autosegment from nasalizing the initial /b/ of 'pot' in (141b), it is assumed that this and other initial oral obstruents in root morphemes will have a *pre-specified* [-nasal] in their segmental matrix. In other words, they are *neutral* with respect to the nasal tier. The archisegments, on the other hand, will be [o nasal], segmentally, since they will receive their nasal specification either by association with the [+NAS] autosegment or by default [-nasal] specification.

In order to appreciate what an underlying representation might look like, with its many blanks to be filled in with default values, consider the noun [gɔ̀nɔ̀], represented underlyingly as in (142).

(142)   [+NAS]

x	x	x	x
+cons	-cons	+cons	-cons
-son	+son	(o son)	+son
-cont	+cont	(o cont)	+cont
-nasal	(o nasal)	(o nasal)	(o nasal)
+voice	+voice	(o voice)	+voice
+high	-high	-high	-high
-low	(o low)	-low	(o low)
+back	+back	-back	+back
-round	+round	-round	+round
-ant	-ant	+ant	-ant
-cor	-cor	+cor	-cor

The segmental matrices in (142) have a number of blanks. The two vowels, which are identical, are not specified for either nasality or for the feature [low]. The nasality will, of course, be specified by the [+NAS] autosegment. The non-high vowel will then be specified automatically as [+low] since we cannot have [ō] in Gokana. The initial consonant is completely specified. The archisegment /D/ is not specified for [son], [cont] or [nasal], since these are the features whose values will depend upon whether there is a [+NAS] autosegment or not. (The feature [voice] has been tentatively left unspecified only because there is some question whether words such as 'dance' are pronounced [zob] or [zop^o] (both probably acceptable), though it is equally plausible to assume [+voice] and a rule of final devoicing.) Recall that /D/ will be realized as [n] if nasalized, as [r] if oral and intervocalic, or as [l] if oral and not intervocalic. An occasional pronunciation [d] is heard in certain environments, e.g. [el ni] ~ [ed ni] 'more than you'.

I would like to suggest the following nasal mapping procedure to follow the OCR: (i) Nasal mapping applies by *morpheme*, associating each [+NAS] to the first WU of the morpheme. (ii) This is followed by the rightward iterative association of the [+NAS] autosegment onto all WU's within the word domain (see below).

This association of [+NAS] by morpheme to each initial WU is required to account for the invariant (non-alternating) instrumental suffix [-mā] seen earlier in (53). Recall the form [kpɔ́ɔ́-mā] 'cut with', where the nasality of the suffix must not be assigned to the vowel of the verb root /kpɔ́/ 'cut'. This is accomplished in (143).

(143)

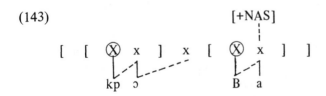

As can be seen, there is a single operation of the OCR within both the root morpheme 'cut' and the non-root (suffix) morpheme 'with'. There is, in addition, a floating WU appearing between the morphemes which is characteristic of this construction, as we saw in (56) above. The verb root in (143) has no nasal autosegment, while the suffix does. In order that the [+NAS] not be assigned to the first WU of the verb form (thereby nasalizing the entire string), it is necessary to stipulate that it is assigned to its own morpheme. This is captured in the above nasal mapping procedure, though it could also have been accounted for if we simply assumed that this exceptionally has its [+NAS] autosegment pre-associated.

Note that clitic pronouns such as /ÉĒ/ 'him/her' and /v̄ā/ 'them' will not have a [+NAS] autosegment, while the clitic pronouns [m] 'me' and [nī] 'you sg.' do:

(144) a.   [+NAS]   b.   [+NAS]

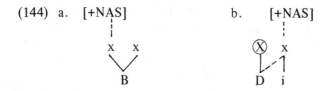

In (144a) I have reinterpreted the first person singular clitic pronoun as a geminate labial archiphoneme with a [+NAS] autosegment. The dotted line indicates the initial nasal association which is followed, of course, by the extension of the [+NAS] association to the second WU. In (144b) I have set up the alveolar archiphoneme /D/ and the vowel /i/, with the morpheme also having a [+NAS] autosegment. This [+NAS] associates onto the one WU remaining after the OCR applies, as seen. Neither of these clitics may nasalize a preceding vowel because the [+NAS] spreading rule applies from left to right only. Thus, even the epenthetic vowel [i] in forms such as [aè dìv-im] 'he hit me' is not nasalized, since the nasality of the clitic is on its right. In [aè mɔ̃n-ĩm] 'he saw me', on the other hand, the epenthetic vowel does get nasalized, because there is a [+NAS] morpheme to its left.

The value of any analysis of nasality in Gokana will depend not only on its ability to predict the distribution of nasality within the lexical morphology, but also its on its ability to account for the spreading of nasality post-lexically. Consider, first, the forms in (145).

(145) a.   /aè BƆ̀Di ÉĒ/   →   [aè mɔ̃n- ɛ̃ɛ̃]   'he saw him'
       b.   /aè BƆ̀Di ṽa/   →   [aè mɔ̃n-va]   'he saw them'
       c.   /aè BƆ̀Di óD/   →   [aè mɔ̃n ʔól]   'he saw the farm'

In (145a) the clitic pronoun 'him/her' does not have a [+NAS] autoseg-ment of its own, but receives a [+NAS] specification from the preceding nasal verb form (cf. aè dìv-ee 'he hit him', where the verb 'hit' lacks this [+NAS] autosegment and the clitic pronoun surfaces as oral). We can ac-count for this post-lexical nasal spreading if we simply have the cliticiza-tion process define a post-lexical word domain. That is, nasal spreading is a word level rule and will thus apply within this domain whenever it is created, i.e. when created lexically, as we have seen, and when created post-lexically, as in (145a).

In (145b), however, there is no such spreading when the clitic is [va] 'them'. There are several ways to account for this fact. First, and least preferred, one could stop this pronoun from cliticizing, thereby requiring it to remain in a separate word domain. The nasal spreading rule would thus not apply, because it is restricted to applying within the *same* word domain. The cliticization process could therefore be made sensitive to the phonological shape of the clitic: cliticization would apply only if the pronoun in question began with a non-branching WU, i.e. only if it was not of the form CV. In this case, cliticization would be phonologically predictable and, in fact, no need would have to be made to cliticization at all. This proposal, while appealing, does not account for all of the facts (see below).

A second possible approach would be to follow a suggestion made originally to me by Nick Clements. In root morphemes beginning with an oral obstruent, this consonant would have an opaque [-NAS] autosegment. Thus, in (145b), the initial /v/ would itself block the spreading of the preceding [+NAS] autosegment by means of its underlying pre-linked [-NAS] association. The interpretation I have given to opaque associations earlier has been that such segments also have a corresponding pre-specified feature, in this case, a [-nasal] specification. This analysis could also account for the failure of a [+NAS] autosegment to cross into a following word domain, if each such word began with an opaque [-NAS] association. This would affect the underlying representation of words such as 'farm' in (145c), which we have assumed to have no initial consonant. The glottal stop in oral and nasal vowel-initial *stem* morphemes would have to be underlying and would have to have an opaque [-NAS] association when occurring in an oral stem. Clitics such as 'him/her' in (145a) would remain vowel-initial underlyingly, though they would receive a glottal stop phrase-initially by rule (42). This glottal would itself have to have an opaque [-NAS] association, violating the claim I made earlier that there can be no opaque epenthesis.

A third approach will therefore be taken. I will assume that post-lexical nasal spreading may extend a preceding [+NAS] association only onto a *non-branching* WU. That is, if the following WU dominates a CV sequence, post-lexical nasal spreading will not take place. Consider the data in (146).

(146) a. /B̄ # gà/   →   [ŋgà]   'needle'
       b. [aè mɔ̀n ɔ̃ tɔ?]   'he saw your (sg.) house'
       c. [aè mɔ̀n ?o tɔ?]   [idem]

In (146a) we see that the diminutive prefix involves an underlying /B/ archisegment and a [+NAS] autosegment, but that this [+NAS] does not spread onto the following WU. This is explained by the fact that the latter dominates a CV and hence branches. The alternative that the initial /g/ of /gà/ 'skewer' has an opaque [-NAS] association will not account for the alternative pronunciations of 'he saw your sg. house' in (146), however. In (146b), the /o/ 'your' of /o tɔ/ 'your house' has undergone post–lexical nasal spreading since its WU does not branch. In (146c), on the other hand, a glottal stop has been inserted instead and the resulting WU geometry blocks post–lexical nasal spreading. The temptation is to refer to (146b) as a cliticized form (which it is) and (146c) as a non–cliticized form (which it also is), and then to say that nasal spreading is restricted to the post–lexical word domain created by the cliticization process only. This would seem to be contradicted, however, by (146a), which I believe we would want to call a post–lexical word. Thus, unless we are to distinguish between post–lexical words created through procliticization and those created through encliticization, we will have to abandon the domain explanation of post–lexical nasal spreading.

To recapitulate, lexical nasal spreading is 'free", i.e. it extends to all available WU's to the right of the initial [+NAS] association. Post–lexical nasal spreading is restricted to WU's which do not branch. Note, finally, that there is at least one exceptional morpheme which should, but does not undergo post–lexical nasal spreading (cf. 160):

(147) a. m̀m̄ tú nwín eé   'I will take a child + EMPH'
      b. m̀m̄ tú n m èé   'I will take an animal +EMPH'
      c. m̀m̄ tú kùn é   'I will take a basket + EMPH'

The emphatic marker has three different pronunications, depending on the tone of the preceding word (H, M and L, respectively, in (147)), but it is never pronounced nasally and hence never becomes [ɛ̃] or [ɛ̃ɛ̃]. This will be accounted for by saying that it exceptionally has vowels which are pre-specified as [-nasal]. It is significant that this morpheme also does not acquire an initial glottal stop.

8.2. The mapping of tone in Gokana

Having demonstrated how nasal mapping is to take place in Gokana, we can turn to the mapping of tonal melodies in this language. It has been pointed out already that verb feet may map at most two distinct tones as a melody. Thus, in (4) we saw the mapping of a HL melody. Of the possible combinations of the three tones, H, M and L, only the following mono- and bi-tonal melodies are attested: H, M, L, HM, HL, MH and ML. I indicate H, M and L, rather than HH, MM, and LL, for reasons which will become apparent. The two conspicuously missing melodies are *LH and *LM. I will show that LH does not occur at least in part because at an underlying level the second tone may not be H. (I will, for instance, reanalyze the MH melody as a H melody having a lowering effect on the first WU to which it associates.) The LM melody, on the other hand, does not occur because there is a simplification of this melody to M (via the deletion of the L), as we saw in (30).

For the purpose of our discussion on the mapping of verb tones, the following table of paradigms will serve as reference:

UNDERLYING VERB FORM		O TENSE	P TENSE	F TENSE
sa L	'to choose'	à sa ò saà ò saì	aè sà oò sà oò sai	àé sa òó sa òó sai
tu H	'to take'	à tú ò túù ò túì	aè tù oò tù oò tui	àé tú òó tú òó túi
bii LM	'to squeeze'	à bii ò bìì ò biìrìì	aè bii oò bii oò biirii	àé bii òó bii òó biirii
sii HM	'to catch'	à síi ò síì ò síìrìì	aè sii oò sii oò siirii	àé síi òó síi òó síirii
diB-i L	'to hit'	à dib ò divì ò divìì	aè dìb oò dìb oò divii	àé dib òó dib òó divii
koD-i H	'to call'	à kórí ò kórì ò kórìì	aè korí oò korí oò korii	àé kórí òó kórí òó kórii
da-Da L	'to pick up'	à darà ò darà ò daràì	aè dàrà oò dàrà oò darai	àé darà òó darà òó darai
Dǎ-Da H	'to find sth. lost'	à náná ò nánà ò nánàì	aè naná oò naná oò nanai	àé náná òó náná òó nánai
Dee-Da L	'to praise'	à leèrà ò leèrà ò leèràì	aè lèèrà oò lèèrà oò leerai	àé leèrà òó leèrà òó leera
too-Da H	'To carry on head'	à tóórá ò tóòrà ò tóòràì	aè toorá oò toorá oò toorai	àé tóórá òó tóórá òó tóorai
kɛ-DE L M	'to hang sth., deceive'	à kɛrɛ ò kɛrè ò kɛrèì	aè kɛrɛ oò kɛrɛ oò kɛrɛi	àé kɛrɛ òó kɛrɛ òó kɛrɛi
koD-E L L	'to sift'	à korè ò korè ò korèì	aè kòrè oò kòrè oò korei	àé korè òó korè òó korei
ZoG-E H L	'to show'	à zógè ò zógè ò zógèì	aè zogè oò zogè oò zogei	àé zógè òó zógè òó zogei

In this table verb forms of varying underlying tonal and segmental shape are given in the zero (0), past (P) and future (F) tenses. For each verb there are three rows of forms representing, respectively, third person singular, second person singular and second person plural subject pronominal forms. The reason for this kind of display will become evident. I shall begin by discussing the nature of underlying verb forms.

(a) The verb forms given in the first column consist either of a verb root alone or of a verb root plus one suffix (separated from the root by a hyphen). As seen, the verb root itself has either H or L tone. That is, in this analysis there are no underlying M tone verb roots. The M that is found in LM and HM combinations, e.g. 'to squeeze' and 'to catch' is probably a historical suffix - and it may be necessary to view it this way even in present-day Gokana (see below).[29] In addition, there are two "grade suffixes" (recall the foot structure of verbs in (33)) -i and -Da, both of which are toneless. The reason for identifying these as grade suffixes is that they have no meaning in themselves, but rather are part of the lexical entry. Other derivational suffixes may be added to these forms (causing the grade suffix to fall), including the transitive suffix -È in 'to sift' and 'to show', the intransitive suffix -a (toneless) seen in (52a), and the -Bã instrumental suffix seen in (53), which sometimes loses its L tone by a predictable rule. The suffix -DE with M tone in 'to hang sth.' is also analyzed as a grade suffix and has an exceptional M tone. It also oddly only attaches to CV verb roots whose vowel is /ɛ/, cf. dɛ -rɛ 'to cover', bɛ -rɛ 'to lean'. It seems to add a meaning of 'positioning' some object. Since the resulting verb is transitive, /-DE/ may be related either to /-E/ or to /-Da/, both of which are transitivizers, but both of which have different tonal properties from /-DE/.

It will be noted that I have analyzed 'to hit' with a final /-i/ grade suffix, although this vowel is realized only in the 0 tense. (It should not be confused with the second person plural subject suffix /-ii/, which may appear in all tenses.) It turns out that all surface CVC verb roots have a lexical L, while all surface CVC-i occurring outside the 0 tense have a H tone verb root. This complementary distribution is accounted for by positing the grade suffix in L tone verbs like 'to hit', but in deleting it if it both follows a L tone verb root and if its WU does not have a tone. In the zero tense, as seen in (148), there is an extra L tone inflectional morpheme occurring last in the verb form if the subject is either first or second person:

(148)   m̀ div-ì 'I hit'   è div-ì 'we hit'
       ò div-ì 'you sg. hit'   ò div-ìì 'you pl. hit'
       á dib 'he/she hits'   bà dib 'they hit'

As can be seen in the form [ò saà] 'you choose' (cf. [à sa] 'he chooses'), if the verb forms consists only of a CV root, an extra WU is introduced. In longer verb forms, however, such as ò tóòrà 'you sg. carry (on head)', the L tone is present without an extra WU. In all tenses the second person plural morpheme /-ii/ is realized according to the rules of Gokana that we have seen: by the DGR in (25) the vowel will degeminate if following a vowel, and by the D-epenthesis rule in (99), either a [r] or a [n] will precede the geminate vowel if it is in turn preceded by a geminate vowel

(b) We are now ready to address the major properties of the tone patterns in the table. First, a minor observation. In aè tù 'he took and oò tù 'you sg. took', the H tone verb /tú/ 'take' merges with the L tone verb /sà/ 'choose'. As seen in forms where there is a following suffix, e.g. oò tú-i 'you pl. took', or as seen in sentences where there is a word following the verb, e.g. aè tú nɔm 'he took an animal', the L tone in aè tú is the result of a specific lowering rule affecting H tone CV verb forms in this tense when occurring before pause.[30] For the purpose of our tone mapping rules, then, we shall ignore this late rule and consider the two past tense forms to have a H tone on /tú/, as it appears when not pre-pausal.

Comparing the P and F tenses only, which are marked, respectively, by the /è/ or /é/ following the subject (where /o/ + /e/ fuses as [oo]), we see that there are considerable tonal differences: a verb form which begins L in the P tense will begin M in the F tense, and a verb form which begins H in the F tense will begin M in the P tense. Because of verbs such as bii 'to squeeze' and kɛrɛ 'to hang', which begin M in both tenses, the generalizations have to be stated as I have just done. The 0 tense has the same tonal properties as the F tense, as far as the initial tone is concerned, the only difference being the complication introduced by the first and second person subjects in the 0 tense, which we have just seen illustrated for 'hit' in (148). I will assume that these differences in initial tone are due to a floating tone that precedes the verb forms, and which is inserted according to the verb tense/construction type. In the case of the P tense, I will propose that a pre-verb M tone is spelled out when the verb root is H; in the F tense a pre-verb M tone is spelled out when the verb root is L. We therefore can attribute the initial M of L tone verbs in the 0 and F tenses to this pre-verb M tone, and the initial M of H tone verbs in the P tense to the pre-verb M tone (as per the rules that are formalized below).[31]

The above statement concerning initial M tones does not apply in the case of the verbs bii 'to squeeze' and kɛrɛ 'to hang' or to the P tense L tone verbs which have the second person plural suffix /-ii/ (with its M tone). Whether from the lexical representation, as in the case of the above two cited verbs, or from the inflectional morphology, as in forms like oò leera-i 'you pl. praised' (from a L verb root, a toneless grade suffix, and the M tone second person plural subject suffix), a LM tonal sequence within a verb foot is simplified by deleting the L. This is because the LM contour is not an acceptable melody at the foot level in Gokana. As we shall see below, it may be created post-lexically, but even here there are some possibilities for simplifying it to a M which potentially downsteps. I shall therefore assume that this L deletion rule applies prior to the initial tone assignment rule and that in forms such as oò leerai, the L of the verb root rather than associating and then disassociating, is deleted before any association is possible.

A similar deletion rule affects the M of the second person plural suffix when it occurs in the 0 tense. As seen in forms such as ò síì-rìì 'you pl. catch', which should be compared with the corresponding future form òó síi-rii 'you pl. will catch', we obtain a HL melody, rather than a HM one. Thus, the H + M + L sequence of tones which are accumulated from the H verb root, the M second person plural suffix and the L 0 tense tone assigned when the subject is first or second person is simplified by deleting the M tone. This was exemplified also in (8) above. Since the segments of the M tone suffix /-ii/ survive, rather than being replaced by the L tone suffix of the 0 tense, we have a case of morpheme concatenation followed by a simplification of the tonal melody.[32]

A different situation obtains in cases where a grade suffix is "replaced" by a derivational suffix. In this case the latter suffix replaces both the segments *and* the tone of the grade suffix. Thus, consider the following examples:

(149) a. aè kɛrɛ nu   'he hung (carried) sth. (on his shoulder/ by his neck)'

       b. aè kɛ̀rà nu   'he hung (sth.) up'

       c. aè kɛ̀ɛ̀à nu   'it hung/it dropped'

The M-M form kɛrɛ 'hang' is the one presented as underlying in the table of verb forms. It was suggested that the verb root /kɛ̀/, which never appears by itself, has an underlying L tone, and that the "contactive" suffix -DE has a M tone. With the LM simplifying to M by the L deletion rule mentioned up two paragraphs, the remaining M can then map onto the two WU's of this verb form.

When either the transitive suffix /-Da/ or the intransitive suffix /-a/ "replace" the grade suffix /-DE/, the M tone of the latter is also not found. Instead, the replacive suffixes observed in (149b) and (149c) have no underlying tone of their own: the all L melody seen in these forms comes from the mapping of the lexical L of the verb root onto all of the WU's of the verb foot. This, then, is the evidence for the underlying L of the root 'hang', and also for the L of the LM melody of bii 'to squeeze' and the H of the HM melody of síi 'to catch'. The intransitive forms of these verbs are pronounced [bììà] and [sííá] (optionally with a slight [y] as discussed in (101)). In these forms it is the L or H of the verb root that spreads onto all of the WU's, since the intransitive suffix /-a/ is toneless.

We are now ready to see how the tonal mapping takes place. I shall demonstrate the different rules in answer to the following question: in àé dib 'he will hit', where there is a M floating before the verb in this tense followed by a L root tone, why do we obtain a M, rather than a ML on the verb? Since dib (coming from diBi) has two WU's, why can't this ML melody be mapped to yield *àé dīb? Note first in (150) that the final consonant of a CVC verb (or noun, for that matter) must be allowed to be tone bearing, since it can receive the H tone that precedes either a locative or temporal expression:

(150) a. àé dīb̄ niʔeí   'he will hit (it) today'
       b. àé mɔ̄ń niʔeí   'he will see (it) today'

In fact, the H tone [ń] is rendered syllabic as per the discussion in section 4.1. Its WU is protected from deletion by the MCR in (23), since the H tone assigned by the following temporal adverb niʔeí 'today' is not identical to the M tone of the verb. Further evidence that the final consonant must have a WU of its own is seen in (151).

(151) a. àé sā́ niʔeí ~ àé sá niʔeí   'he will choose (it) today'
       b. *àé díb niʔeí / *àé mɔ́n niʔeí

In (151a) it is observed that when the M tone verb has the structure CV, it may either be realized with a short MH rising tone or with a simple H tone. The first realization is the only contradiction to the generalization in Gokana that only one tone may be associated to a single WU. I assume that the association of the temporal H derives the MH rising tone, but that this MH contour may optional simplify by disassociating the M, leaving a simple H tone on the verb. (151a) also shows that this "juncture tone", as I called it in Hyman (1982a), does not have a WU of its own, in contrast to the WU accompanying the L associative or genitive tone seen in (22). The crucial point is derived from the unacceptable tonal forms in (151b). When the M tone verb has the structure CVC, the MH rising tone seen in (150) may not simplify to a H. The reason is straightforward, if we assume that the final consonant has its own WU: the M remains on the WU of the CV, while the temporal H goes on the WU of the final C. No simplification is possible, because we do not have two tones (MH) linked to a single WU.

However, the above constitutes a potential complication, since the final C appears to be weightless early in the derivation, but weight-bearing later in the derivation. The forms àé dib 'he will hit' and àé mɔn 'he will see' appear to demonstrate that the final C does not have a WU, otherwise the ML melody would have been assigned to yield *àé dĩb and *àé mɔ̃ñ.

There are several possible approaches to tone mapping in Gokana. I will therefore outline the one that seems to be the simplest to me and which, at the same time, can get us out of the above dilemma. I assume the following ordered statements and rules.

(a) Taking the underlying verb tones to consist of the tone of the verb root and the tone of any suffixes, one first deletes the L of any LM sequence.

(b) Introducing the possible pre-verbal M tone referred to earlier, one now introduces a rule deleting the medial tones of any tri- or quadritonal sequence (cf. the above discussion and note 32).

(c) The OCR applies followed by the rule that deletes the [i] grade suffix in a verb form having only one L tone.[33]

(d) Tone mapping takes place with the first tone being assigned to the first WU and, if there is one, the second tone being assigned to the second WU. Any remaining WU's receive an extended association from the rightmost tone.

(e) Two patch-up rules apply: one changing (152a) to (152b) and one changing (153a) to (153b).

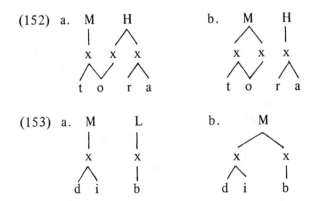

The mapping rules predict that 'he carried on the head' will be pronounced *aè toórá, with the M on the first WU and the H on the second two WU's, as in (152a). The correct form, however, is aè toorá. A MH sequence *is* permitted on a CVV sequence in Gokana, but not when this sequence is followed by another WU associated to the same H. Thus, the rule required to change (152a) to (152b) is formalized as in (154).

(154) M   H

x   x   x

This rule says that when a M WU is followed by a H associated onto two
WU's the M extends its association to the right, disassociating the H. Note
that there is no need to refer to the shape of the WU's in question, since
the only time when a M-H-H sequence will be derived by the above rules
on three WU's is when the verb form has the shape CVVCV or CVVV
(cf. baè beeá 'they judged each other'). Since the first two WU's will always dominate a single vowel matrix, i.e. since there will always be a
geminate vowel, rule (154) represents a case where the tonal representation is adjusted to reflect in a one-to-one way the vowel representations
characterizing the same mediating WU's.

Turning to (153a), we see that the mapping of a ML melody will result
in the incorrect form *àé dīb 'he will hit'. In order for this to correctly
surface as àé dib in (153b), the patch-up rule in (155) is necessary:

(155) M   Ⓛ

x   x

[+cons]

This rule says that when the L of a ML melody is associated onto a WU
which dominates only a [+cons] segment, the L is deleted and the M on
the left extends its association onto the second WU. This rule takes place
prior to the introduction of the post-lexical juncture tones to the right
of the word, since, as we saw in (21b) and (24a) above, the L associative
morpheme will cause the final C of a CVC word to surface as syllabic
with L tone as a later development.

After the operations of (a) – (e) above, the floating junctural H is assigned to the preceding word, which may be a noun or a verb. This results
in the disassociation of the tone of the last WU of this word, unless, as
was seen in (151a), the word has only one WU, in which case the disassociation is optional. The last rule of relevance is the MCR in (23), which
applies in cases where the second WU of a CVC form has the same tone
as the preceding WU.

Before leaving the junctural H tone of temporals and locatives, consider
the data in (156).

(156) a. gὲ 'knife'   : aè mòn gε ni?eí   'he saw a knife today'
       b. kɔ̀ɔ̀ 'hen'   : aè mòn k ɔ̀ɔ̀/k ɔ̀ɔ̀ ni?eí 'he saw a hen today'

    c. kàn 'cloth'   : aè mɔ̀n kàn̄/kan niʔeí 'he saw cloth today'
    d. fìnì 'monkey' : aè mɔ̀n fìni/fini niʔeí 'he saw a monkey today'

Here we see that the junctural tone comes out as a M when the preceding tone is L. The examples involve four nouns of different phonological structure. When the noun is CV, as in (156a), the modification is from L to M. Presumably the L disassociated by the H will still be available to change the H to a M (there are no LH sequences in Gokana except across word boundaries). When the L tone noun has more than one WU, two different possibilities are observed: either L–M or M–M. This is true, whether we have a CVV noun, as in (156b), a CVC noun, as in (156c), or a CVCV noun, as in (156d). In the examples in (156) the nouns in question are preceded by a verb with L tone. When the verb has a M tone (because it is a L tone root in the F tense) the following alternatives are observed:

(157) a. àé mɔn 'gɛ niʔeí   'he will see a knife today'
       b. àé mɔn kɔ̄ɔ̄/'kɔ̄ɔ̄ niʔeí   'he will see a hen today'
       c. àé mɔn kàn̄/'kan niʔeí   'he will see cloth today'
       d. àé mɔn fìni/'fini niʔeí   'he will see a monkey today'

In (157a) it is seen that when the L of /gɛ̀/ 'knife' is disassociated by the following juncture tone, its L floats before the noun, conditioning its lowering from H to M, but also remaining to serve as a downstep indicator. I assume Clements and Ford's (1979) analysis of downstep as a floating L in this case, i.e. the sequence mɔ̄n ˋ gɛ̄ in (157a) is pronounced as a M followed by a lowered M. Since the initial M of niʔeí 'today' is realized on the same level as the M of 'knife', it is clear that we are dealing with a downstepped M, rather than a distinct, fourth tone. The same realization is seen in the other sentences in (157): either the M (from H) of the junctural tone goes on the last WU, or it is allowed to spread back to both WU's, thereby causing the underlying L of the noun to float, thereby conditioning downstep. The M vs. 'M opposition is possible in Gokana only after a non–L tone, i.e. after H or (')M. Where longer forms are involved, the junctural M (from H) is allowed to spread leftwards only over a second WU and no more. Thus, compare ò k ɛ̀ɛ̄ɛ̄ī 'you pl. wake (s.o.) up' and ò k ɛ̄ɛ̄ɛ̄ī niʔeí 'you pl. wake (s.o.) up today' (not *ò k ɛ̄ɛ̄ɛ̄ī niʔeí, where the M has spread leftwards onto the first L WU of the verb as well).

8.3. The mapping of vowel harmony in Gokana

The final mapping procedure I would like to discuss in this section concerns vowel harmony. In this section I have been strongly influenced by the work of Clements (1980) and Clements and Sezer (1983). Gokana vowel harmony is limited to the vowels [e, o, ɛ ,ɔ]. The general rule is that different heights among these vowels may not be mixed (but see below).

In the present discussion I shall distinguish between root and non-root morphemes. I shall also assume that the difference between /e/ and /o/, on the one hand, and /ɛ/ and /ɔ/, on the other, is that the former are mid vowels, while the latter are low vowels. We shall see considerable motivation for this interpretation (rather than an interpretation in terms of tense and lax vowels). It is clear, then, that these mid vowels contrast with the corresponding low vowels in root morphemes, as seen in (158).

(158) a. /té/   'tree'   c. /dò/   'to measure'
       b. /tɛ̀/   'father, nest'   d. /dɔ̀/   'to fall'

In root morphemes, as well as non-root morphemes, on the other hand, when there is a [+NAS] specification on the nasal tier, only the [+low] members of the opposition are possible, i.e. [ɛ̃] and [ɔ̃].

Non-root morphemes are much more restricted with respect to this potential opposition. Most suffixes and clitics agree in lowness with the preceding vowel of the root morpheme, as seen in (159).

(159) a. aè sí-e   'he¡ went'
       b. aè dé-è   'he¡ ate'
       c. aè fɛ́ -ɛ̀   'he¡ killed'
       d. aè tú-è   'he¡ took'
       e. aè do-è   'he¡ measured'
       f. aè dɔ -ɛ̀   'he¡ fell'
       g. aè sa-ɛ̀   'he¡ chose'

The forms in (159) involve the logophoric suffix, which has been referred to above as /-ÈÈ/. As seen, it is realized as [+low] after the vowels /ɛ/, /ɔ/ and /a/, but as [-low] after the vowels /i/, /e/, /u/ and /o/. (After *any* nasalized vowel in the root morpheme, this suffix will be realized [ɛ̃].) All of the other verb suffixes and clitics behave identically, e.g. the transitive suffix /-È/ and its variants, the third person singular clitic /-ÉĒ/, and also the focus marker /-É/ which is present when WH-movement has taken place within a clause. Since these forms only occur as suffixes or enclitics it is not possible to know what value of [low] they would take in isolation.

A few non-root morphemes require [-low] even when the rules would predict agreement with the preceding vowel. The most notable of these is the emphatic marker /èé/ that may appear at the end of a clause (cf. (147)):

(160) a. m̀ḿ tú gyáá eé   'I will take yams!'
      b. m̀ḿ tú tɔ èé   'I will take a house!'
      c. m̀ḿ tú gɛ̀ é   'I will take a knife!'

As seen, the tone varies according to the preceding tone: geminate MH after a H, geminate LH after a M, and single H after a L. Not only does the mid vowel remain mid after the above [+low] vowels, but it also does not become nasal by the spreading of the [+NAS]. There would seem, then, to be no alternative to representing this morpheme as opaquely specified as low and [-NAS].[34]

For a few other non-root morphemes, especially pronouns, it is possible to argue for an underlying representation from which the opposite value of [low] is derived. Perhaps the forms in (161) provide some evidence, for example, that the second person singular pronoun is [-low]:

(161) a. ò dɔɔ̀   'you sg. fall'
      b. nɔ́ɔ̃́ dɔɔ̀   'you sg. don't fall'

The negative consists of /n´/ plus a double length of the subject pronoun (cf. à dɔ 'he falls', náá dɔ 'he doesn't fall', etc.). Since the second person subject pronoun is [o] when oral and at the beginning of a clause, perhaps this is evidence that the [-low] variant is basic?[35]

What I would like to suggest is that there is a [LOW] autosegment, and that we have the following distribution of [+LOW] and [-LOW] according to the other features of each vowel, the root vs. non-root distinction, and the nasality parameter:

(a) In root morphemes, the oral vowels /i/, /u/, /e/ and /o/ will have a [-LOW] autosegment, while the oral vowels /ɛ/, /ɔ/ and /a/ will have a [+LOW] autosegment. /i/ and /u/ will be specified as [+high] in their segmental matrix, while the remaining vowels will be specified as [-high].

(b) In non-root morphemes, the vowels /i/ and /u/ will have a [-LOW] autosegment (and a [+high] in their segmental matrix), while the vowel /a/ will have a [+LOW] autosegment (and a [-high] in its segmental matrix). The remaining vowels will be specified only as [-high] and have no autosegment [LOW]. The few exceptions to this will be morphemes such as the emphatic marker /èé/, which will have an opaque [-LOW] specification (see also note 35).

(c) Any morpheme with a [+NAS] autosegment and a [-high] vowel other than /a/ will introduce the [+LOW] autosegment by rule.

(d) Any E/O type vowel not covered by the above will, if not covered by any of the above, receive a default [-low] specification. This may pertain to the second person subject marker in (161a), for instance.

It should be clear that except for (d), any unmarked [LOW] value will be obtained by spreading the [+LOW] or [-LOW] autosegment from left to right until another such autosegment is met. We may start with the [LOW] autosegments as being unassociated, but to be associated *by morpheme*. This will result in almost no ambiguity in where the autosegments associate, since there are only a handful of unidentical vowel sequences within what one might view as a single morpheme, e.g. bíɔ̃ 'nose', vái 'bed', etc. In some cases it is clear that individual WU's may require an *opaque* association as in the exceptional word láo 'cow' (old variety)'.[36]

As an aside, it can be noted that the possibility, if not the requirement, that both [NAS] and [LOW] be associated by morpheme is further evidence for the primacy of the morpheme category, which, as we saw in section 3.3, has taken over certain characteristics more typical of the syllable or the word in other languages.

Chapter 9

Conclusion

The basic outline of a theory of phonological weight has been presented in the preceding sections. Some of the discussion and analyses are more worked out than others, as indeed this study represents work in progress on a very complex aspect of phonological structure. In this final section I would like to present certain speculations on the internal structure of WU's and segments. In particular, I would like to take a closer look at the special status we have given to the feature [cons] and see if some light might be shed on its significance in the statement of weight phenomena and syllabicity.

The feature [cons] is absolutely essential for the theory developed here. It has served as input to the OCR, to MCR's, to the distinction between high vowels and glides, etc. What I would like to put forth as a hypothesis is that the maximal expansion of a single WU can be stated universally as in (162).

(162)

$$
\begin{array}{ccc}
 & \text{x} & \\
\text{[+cons]} & \text{[–cons]} & \text{[+cons]}
\end{array}
$$

In the preceding sections we have seen instances of WU's consisting solely of a [+cons] segment, solely of a [–cons] segment, and also of combinations of these, obeying the order in (162), with each being optional. Thus, we have CV, CC, VC, and CVC WU's. The CC type, for example, was seen in the syllabic liquids of Idoma in (68b). It is probably the right way to talk about the non-initial syllabic sonorants in Berber words such as [ixðm̩] 'he works' for which the following derivation is proposed:

(163)
$$
\begin{array}{ccccccccc}
\text{x} & \text{x} & \text{x} & & \text{x} & \rightarrow & \text{x} & \text{x} \\
| & | & | & \boxed{\text{ə}} & | & & \diagup\diagdown & \diagup\diagup\diagdown \\
\text{i} & \text{x} & \text{d} & & \text{m} & & \text{i \quad x} & \text{ð \quad ə \quad m}
\end{array}
$$

In (163) we have the underlying form with each segment having a WU. The schwa insertion rule in (107) inserts the schwa, as indicated. This is followed now by a MCR, which joins a [+cons] segment to the WU of a preceding [−cons] segment. As seen, this creates a binary WU followed by a ternary one. The final step is the deletion of the schwa, conditioned by the [+son] feature of the [m] (see the discussion surrounding the possible reformulation of schwa insertion in (107′) above). This leaves a WU dominating two [+cons] segments. The question I would like to raise is whether two [+cons] features is necessary or even desirable? Should a version of Leben's (1978) obligatory contour principle force us to have one [+cons]?

The most likely place for such a constraint to hold is in the creation of complex onsets and margins. The universal OCR has given a rationale for the deletion of the WU of a [+cons] segment when followed by a [−cons] one. But why should sequences of [+cons] segments join up under the same WU, whether as an onset or as a margin? Perhaps the reason is that at this stage in the derivation we basically are deriving "complex consonants". Let us turn to the treatment of complex consonants themselves.

Note in (164) that if we assume the representation of an affricate to be two [+cons] segments having one WU a problem arises in the application of the OCR:

(164) a.   b.

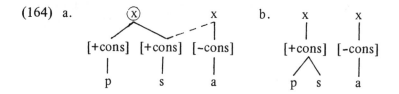

I have purposely chosen a heteroganic affricate so that several feature differences must characterize the two parts of the affricate. When the OCR applies in (164a) only the [+cons] matrix of the /s/ reassociates with the following [−cons] WU. We could propose a special convention that complex segments must maintain their unitary nature, but this would not be very satisfying. The derivation in (164a) would suggest that the unmarked state would be for the OCR to create a floating [+cons] segment, here the /p/, which might conceivably prefer to attach to a *preceding* [−cons] WU. But this is rarely, if ever the case. If we had a language with affricates in initial position only – the same sequences belonging to two different "syllables" intervocalically – we would almost certainly treat the so-called affricate as a sequence of two real segments, i.e. each with its own WU.

The tentative solution is seen in (164b). Here we have the /p/ and the /s/ both reporting to a single [+cons]. Thus, when the OCR applies, the complex [+cons] entity reassociates as one to the following WU. Now let us consider the other language where /p/ and /s/ each have their own [+cons] feature matrix, each with their own WU. The /s/ will automatically join the WU of a following vowel, here /a/. Now, if this language were to have an onset adjunction rule adding the /p/ to the -sa- WU, we would obtain (165a). The question is: can this be distinct in any language from the representation in (165b)?

(165) a.

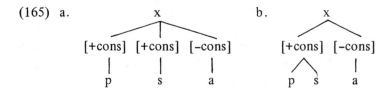

I would like to claim that these representations are non-distinct and that therefore (165a) should, if ever created, at a late stage in the derivation be converted to (165b).[37] The reason is simple: the end-point of the phonological derivation should serve as the input to the phonetic realization rules. In both (165a) and (165b) we have one WU with the same sets of features, save the different number of [+cons] specifications in the onset. The only way two [+cons]'s could be distinct from one is if they belonged to different WU's. In other words, the OCP of Leben is valid at the level of the WU. We cannot have two H tones associated onto the same WU in sequence, nor should we have two [+cons] features in sequence when dominated by the same x. If we follow through with this notion, then the output of (163) must be a single [+cons] dominating a ðm sequence. Within this sequence the [m] will be "syllabic" because it is more sonorant than the [ð].

The major argument, then, for the OCP is *phonetic reality*. It doesn't matter for the phonetics whether [ps] came to be an onset from a single WU (in which case it was underlyingly an affricate) or from two WU's (in which case it was a sequence of two consonants). This distinction is important only at an earlier stage of the phonological derivation. Once within the same WU the distinction disappears.

A similar argument can be made for the so-called short diphthongs that have been mentioned. While they have been talked about as having two [-cons] matrices dominated by the same WU, perhaps they should begin with a single [-cons] dominating the two matrices. Vowels having their own underlying WU's which might come together later in the derivation by rule, would also at a late stage be subjected to the OCP as well.

What I am suggesting is that certain distinctions which are phonological in nature must not be carried through to the phonetics. Whether something is a /ky/ sequence or a /kʸ/ is a question of structural interest only. The CV tier does not make the same prediction about the phonetics as does the proposal I am making here. Thus, Clements' gliding rule in Luganda given in (120) claims that /kia/ becomes [k^{y}aa], although the latter is not distinguishable from [kyaa], which would be CCVV in the CV approach.

It should be noted that there is considerable evidence for the need of separating out the [cons] feature as opposed to all other features. Consider, for example, the representation of [ĩvý] 'rain' in Kom, a Grassfields Bantu language. The first WU is the vowel prefix /i-/; the second has the /v/ serving as both onset (non-syllabic) and nucleus (syllabic). Similarly, languages may require homorganic glides before WU's which would otherwise begin with /i/ or /u/. The two situations would be represented in this framework as in (166).

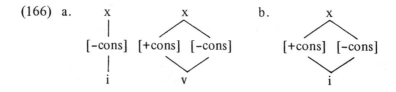

I have left the strident vowel as [-cons], though it is perhaps possible that the [-cons] is dropped as well.[38] Since in representations such as (166) we have a single segment /v/ or /i/ attaching to two [cons] features, it should not be too hard to accept the possibility of more than one segment assigned to a single [+cons] or [-cons], as I have suggested.

Adherence to the maximal template for WU's in (162) is a late phenomenon. I leave open the question of whether other features will have to obey a late OCP or not. It strikes me as likely that some of the feature linking that has been proposed for certain assimilations (see, for instance, Steriade 1982), essentially joins segments to the same [cons] feature, though more research will be necessary before the implications of such a move might be understood. I would like to assert, as a final point, that even if we accept a very special status for [cons], we are not resorting back to a CV tier equivalent. That is, we are still proposing more than the substitution of the features [+cons] and [-cons] for the features [-syll] and [+syll]. The proposal here differs crucially from one which would keep the C's and V's (or which would reinterpret them as values of [cons]) and then add a mora tier, because it is the weight tier that is the core, while the CV tier would remain the core (i.e. the mediator of tiers) in this restatement. Of course, if the C's and V's were reinterpreted as [+cons] and [-cons] and if the "mora tier" were considered the core, we would arrive at the same proposal I've made in this study.[39]

Notes

1. It is possible, however, for there to be a C.V structure if the C and the V belong to different words which belong to different phrases. The automatic CV syllabification is universal only in level 1 word formation processes and may not necessarily be observed in level 2 morphology or post-lexically. Of course, many languages continue to syllabify across word and phrase boundaries, in which case the universal lexical rule of syllabification is obeyed at several or all levels.

2. Another argument for syllables is that the syllable may be a feature-bearing unit, e.g. for tone, as has been claimed for some languages. In this case it serves neither as input to the construction of higher prosodic structures nor as input to the grouping of smaller units into constituents. Instead, its function is to allow the mapping of a feature onto it.

3. I am not counting the subparts of the syllable (onset, rime etc.) as hierarchical units distinct from the syllable. Also, the CV tier definitely mediates between the segmental features and the syllable but does not constitute a hierarchical unit in the sense to be developed here.

4. One occasionally finds references to the attraction of a stress by a CVC syllable, e.g. Araucanian (Echeverría and Contreras 1965:134), Gutob-Remo (Zide 1965:44), and Capanahua (Safir 1979). While these cases may have an alternative interpretation, the fact remains that no language has a rule of the shape "stress the last CVC syllable of a word; if there is no CVC syllable, stress the first syllable of the word", etc. For the same reason, the Spanish prohibition of antepenultimate stress when the penultimate syllable is closed is not considered to be a true counterexample.

5. The three possible feature combinations not represented in (11) are: [+cons, +syll, -son], which would be a syllabic obstruent; [-cons, +syll, -son], which might be a voiceless vowel; and [-cons, -syll, -son], which might be a voiceless glide or possibly, the glottal stop.

6. The only possibility for the second part of a genitive construction to begin with a vowel occurs when the possessor noun is itself modified by the proposed possessives o 'your sg.' and a 'his/her', as in nɔ̄m ʔo kà 'the animal of your mother'. As seen, a glottal stop is inserted, since /o/ 'your' occurs after a left bracket (see rule (42) below). However, there is an optional readjustment rule that allows the bracket to be deleted when the vowel-initial morpheme is a non-root one. In this case there is no glottal stop and the tonal realization is nɔ̄m 'ōō kà. The two interesting features of this second possibility are both the presence of the downstep (the tonal sequence involved is M followed by a downstepped M) and the lengthening of the vowel of the possessive pronoun. Both can be explained if the WU carrying the L tone receives its vowel features *from the right* in cases where the bracket deletion readjustment has taken place. We thus have the following derivation:

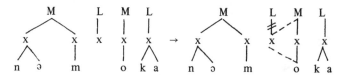

The form on the left is what we obtain after the OCR and tone mapping (by morpheme). The form on the right results from the association of the vowel /o/ to the possessive WU to its left. This creates a long vowel with a LM contour. This contour simplifies as a M by having the M associate onto the preceding WU, thereby disassociating the L (cf. also the examples in (157) below). The floating L tone now is interpreted as a downstep marker on the following M tone (cf. Clements and Ford 1979, who propose this interpretation of downstep). The one remaining rule that must apply is the MCR in (23) which must delete the WU of the /m/ of 'animal' since it has the same tone as the preceding WU.

7. Consonant clusters do arise post-lexically both across clitic and full–word boundaries.

8. The initial consonant may be the glottal stop, which I propose to insert, however by rule (42). One could start with it as underlying, since the only argument for inserting the glottal stop before a *stem*–initial vowel is that it is clearly inserted in the case of higher level left–brackets (e.g. before a vowel that appears immediately after a phrase [ ). (Cf. also the discussion concerning nasalization and the glottal stop in (145c).)

9. Words which have a L-M contour in isolation invariably are compounds, e.g. kpò–dɛm 'stone' and pà–sáā 'leaf'. A L-M sequence is sometimes found on a foot in context where the L belongs to the foot and the M is a juncture tone (cf. 156 below).

10. Note that there is a problem in determining whether these and other reduplicated forms constitute one foot or two. The mapping of the tonal melody (ML for L tone verbs, HL for H tone verbs) indicates that they are a single foot. The ability of having the C_i consonant in a non–initial position, however, would on the face of it seem to argue that we have two feet – or perhaps a foot preceded by something outside the foot (if not a foot in its own right). Of course, if we follow Marantz's (1982) proposals for reduplication, the same C_i consonant will be associated onto both [+cons] slots in the forms in (34) and the generalizations on the distribution of consonantal units within the foot can be maintained.

11. The other major possibility is reintroducing a feature such as [voc] to take the place of feature [syll]. This has been proposed by a number of phonologists, e.g. Clements and Keyser (1981) subsequently abandoned in Clements and Keyser (1983), Cairns and Feinstein (1982), Lowenstamm (1981). This feature would be [+voc] for syllabic sonorant consonants and vowels and [-voc] for non–syllabic consonants and glides. Since it is my desire to attribute syllabicity to prosodic structure, the proliferation of features, especially [voc], which is the feature [syll] in disguise, is to be avoided.

12. Austin includes CVG syllables as heavy, though it is not clear whether the "G" should be treated as a vowel or as a consonant. In any case, other CVC syllables, e.g. CVr, are definitely light.

13. Martin points out that between words it *is* possible to get a sequence of syllabic nasal followed by a vowel, e.g. naiken # aile 'a Chinese village'. I attribute this to the stronger boundary that occurs in this and comparable forms. It should be recalled that the OCR is universal only in level 1 morphology.

14. Glottal stop insertion is required in word formation, i.e. before a "lexical morpheme" (=stem) which begins with a vowel. In the post-lexical phonology, on the other hand, it is required only when there is a major boundary preceding the vowel. In (38a) and (38c), for example, there is no glottal stop preceding the initial syllabic unit of ŋgà 'needle' and ágbá 'paint'. This is because the initial vowel or syllabic nasal is either a grammatical morpheme (e.g. the nasal is a diminutive prefix; cf. gà 'skewer') or it is exceptional, patterning with other grammatical morphemes preceding the stem. (I have not sought to elicit nouns which begin with a vowel that precedes the foot, but since ágbá 'paint' is the only such noun I have among a corpus of several hundred nouns, it is clearly exceptional. The initial vowel must be pre-foot, because /gb/ can only occur in C_i position, as we saw above.) In the examples in (38) we can propose that the left bracket preceding the whole noun has been deleted as an optional readjustment rule (cf. the forms aè tú ʔŋgà and aè tú ʔágbá which are obtained when the readjustment rule does not apply). The freed up syllabic unit might thus be argued to cliticize onto the preceding word. Note, finally, that suffixes and underlying enclitics may not optionally have a left bracket. Thus we can obtain only nəm á 'that animal' and not *nəm ʔá. (Cf. also note 6.)

15. I consider the glottal stop to be [+cons] (see section 6).

16. I don't think there is much gained by recognizing initial oral stops in words such as know (cf. acknowledge) or gnosis (cf. agnostic), as was entertained in early generative phonology days. However, if a language were to have this property of allowing an underlying initial consonant, e.g. /k,g/, which could only join a preceding syllable, I would try to represent it as a floating consonant, i.e. as weightless (see section 5.1), since the weighted extra–syllabic ones seen in (69) *are* pronounceable. Forms such as the later raise the question of whether English can have syllables containing more than two WU's (cf. also my representation of tests in (72)).

17. In Hyman (1984) I propose that any finally released consonant in English has its own WU. Thus, pronunciations such as [lɪpᵒ] and [hætᵒ] would have only one WU within the one syllable, while pronunciations such as [lupˀ] and [hætˀ] have a second WU. This accounts for the near complementary distrubution between final consonants which exhibit a released/non-released opposition vs. those which exhibit a syllabic/non-syllabic opposition, and predicts that a vowel should be shorter before a non-released consonant than before a released one.

18. My knowledge about Russian yers comes exclusively from discussions with David Pesetsky and from Pesetsky (1979). In this paper Pesetsky shows that yer-lowering must apply cyclically. It is not important for my analysis that there be a following C + yer sequence in order for a yer to be realized, only that there *not* be a following C + non-yer vowel. Since it is hard to justify some yers synchronically (Bernard Comrie, personal communication), this may be an advantage to my analysis, which does not require these particular abstractions.

19. Note that this /D/ is not inserted in (18c) because rule (99) is a lexical process, while cliticization is a post–lexical process (Kiparsky 1982). Thus, cliticization may not feed D–insertion.

20. Where the reverse direction is observed, as in sai becoming saʸi, the association line would of course go from right to left instead. This should not cause any difficulty in interpretation because of the assumptions made about the [cons] specification of vowels vs. glides in section 6.

21. Also acounted for are derivations such as the one converting underlying /t + kkr + m/ to [Θəkkrəm] 'you m. stand up':

As seen, there are two instances of schwa insertion (rule (107)) and there is never any question of separating the two units of the geminate (cf. section 5.5). Thus we obtain a geminate consonant followed by a single consonant.

22.   Saib (1976a:67) discusses cases of where a geminate appears to be broken up by a morphological process, e.g. the zero form of the verb /fżż/ 'to chew', which is pronounced [fəżż] by schwa insertion, has the corresponding "intensive form" /tt + fżaż/, pronounced [ttəfżaż]. It is exactly this kind of "non–concatenative morphology" that McCarthy (1979, 1981) so effectively represents as segmental information on different tiers: the morpheme /a/ in the above example would have its own WU (constituting part of the template, if Berber is analyzeable in terms of binyanim like Arabic), and its vowel features would be on a separate tier. Thus, we have the following representation of this form:

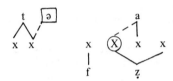

(For the problem with the OCR in this form, see note 39.)

The grammatical morphemes are given above the x's, the lexical root below the x's. Here the schwa insertion rule must look for [+cons] specifications on different tiers in order to know where to apply. This kind of morphological "epenthesis", is thus no counterexample to the generalization made here concerning phonetic epenthesis.

23.   Thus, if a language were to palatalize segments before either /i/ or /y/, where the two differ in [cons], we would be forced to use other features to capture this natural class.

24.   There is, however, no absolute prohibition against four–way branching WU's in French. Annie Rialland has pointed out to me (personal communication) that words such as droit [drwa] require this interpretation. I assume that orthographic oi represents a short diphthong, i.e. that this [wa] sequence starts out with a single WU, rather than two. We therefore have the following derivation of this word (ignoring the final floating /t/):

First the OCR joins the /r/ to the following [−cons] WU. Then an onset adjunction rule joins the /d/ to following WU, resulting in a single WU on the surface. The onset adjunction rule thus is not sensitive to the branching quantity of the x to which it assigns the [+cons] segment, though the "gliding" rule in (119) is.

25.   The problem of specifying a consonant such as /k/ as [−HIGH] is no problem, since this same consonant will have a [+high] in its segmental matrix. Because the autosegments do not override the segmental specifications, /k/ would remain [+high].

26.   Cases of where tones appear to be mapped onto syllables need to be looked at a little more carefully given the concepts developed in this approach. It may be

that the "syllable mapping" is only a derivative of the WU processes. Thus, it may be that tone is mapped onto WU's after the application of a MCR, in which case it may be difficult to tell what is carrying the tone, the WU or the syllable (assuming that there is syllable structure in the language). Tone mapping universally follows the OCR; it may precede or follow possible MCR's depending on the language.

27. If assigning tone to syllables seems more marked than assigning it to WU's, then so does assigning stress to the WU's ("moras") seem more marked than assigning it to syllables. One consequence of assigning stress directly to the WU's is that it ought to be able to distinguish between different *kinds* of WU's, as tone can. For example, there ought to be a sensitivity to consonant types, given the explanation I have provided for what can have reference to what in mapping features. I will leave this question open here, since I have not studied mora-stressing languages.

28. Two additional facts are predicted by the thesis that autosegments may not override segmental specifications: (a) The generalization that consonant types affect tone, but tone does not affect consonant types (Hyman 1973b, Hyman and Schuh 1974) can be attributed to the fact that the tones are the autosegments and the consonant types are prespecified in the segmental matrices. In order for a tone to affect the voicing quality of a consonant, the latter must have a zero specification for voice, to be filled in by the autosegment, presumably. However, the overwhelming tendency among languages without a voicing contrast in obstruents is to represent them in their unmarked, [-voice] specification, lexically. The tone may therefore not override this specification. (b) The definition of a pitch-accent language which I have entertained elsewhere (Hyman 1978) calls for such languages to have a constant tone value assigned to the pitch- or tonal accent. This contrasts with the stress-accent system which has no underlying single tonal specification, but rather alternative melodies to choose from. Now, if these melodies are to be interpreted as the mapping of autosegments onto units unspecified for the tonal features, as has been done by Goldsmith (1976a) and Leben (1976), for English, then in a language which has a prespecified tonal value for its tonal accent (.e.g. a H tone indicated somewhere), it will be impossible for the intonational melody to override it and cause there not to be "a constant tone value". Thus, languages such as Japanese, Somali, Digo etc. do not have intonational melodies which change the underlying H tones to L and vice-versa.

29. I would reconstruct a two-tone system at some pre-Proto-Ogoni stage. As can be seen from the table of verb paradigms, there is no H tone as the second of a two-tone melody. It is possible that 'to squeeze' derives from *LH and 'to catch' from *HH, with a rule that lowered H to M when following another tone. This also accounts for the fact that all suffixes are L, M (from *H) or toneless. Another source of M tone is from a deleted H prefix followed by a L stem.

30. Curiously, this same lowering process takes place before both the focus marker /é/, required when there has been WH-movement in a clause, and the relative marker /á/, as seen in the following sentences:

> nwín ɲáè tù e 'it's the child that took (it)'
> nwín eaè tù a 'the child that took (it)'

The final /é/ or /á/ becomes M after L as if the L-H sequence belonged to the same foot (cf. (156)). However, if the final marker had belonged to the same foot as the verb, /tú/ would not have undergone the prepausal H to L tone-lowering rule.

31. Further evidence that the insertion of the pre-verb tone is sensitive to the tone of the verb root is seen in the following logophoric forms:

aè kɔ aè dɔ-ɛ̀ 'he_i said he_i fell'

aè kɔ aè tu-è 'he_i said he_i took (it)'

In the first sentence the logophoric verb form has a M-L melody despite the fact that the verb root /dɔ̀/ 'fall' has a L tone and the logophoric suffix /ÈÈ/ also has a L tone. A special rule will be required, then, to insert a pre-verb M tone whenever there is this combination of L verb tone and the logophoric suffix. That this rule cannot insert the pre-verb M when the verb tone is H is seen in the second example. In this case the verb root /tú/ 'take' has an underlying H and the logophoric suffix again has an underlying L tone. As seen, we must obtain a M-L melody. This is gotten from the pre-verb M that occurs before H tone verb roots in the P tense. However, the L tone verb 'fall' has a pre-verb M, reminiscent of the O and F tenses (and other tenses), where the corresponding H tone verb is not supposed to have a pre-verb tone at all. Thus, the logophoric suffix in the above examples introduces a pre-verb M for L roots only – and, crucially, leaves the pre-verb M of the P tense present when the verb root is H.

LM M L

32. The example ò bìì-rìì 'you pl. squeeze', from /bi i + ii + /, shows not only that the L deletion rule (before M) must precede the rule deleting internal tones of a tritonal tone melody, but also that we may obtain *four* tones in the verb foot. The two M tones which occur in sequence in this form fuse into one M tone, probably through the deletion of the second M.

33. That the deletion of [i] is sensitive to verbs is seen in the fact that the final [i] remains in L tone nouns such as fìnì 'monkey' and kpòlì 'grave'. Perhaps this is related to the fact that the L tone [i] in verbs does not take a prepausal glottal stop when it *is* pronounced (in the O tense) while the final [i] of nouns such as the above do. On the other hand, verbs such as [kórí?] 'call', whose final [i] is H tone *do* take a glottal stop before pause. The conditioning factors determining whether a final vowel will receive a glottal stop before pause are not difficult to state. They are, however, dependent on so many phonetic and morphological factors that it is hard to see any general pattern covering all cases. Here I have simply speculated that the deletion of the final [i] in verbs may be ultimately related to the failure of such vowels to take glottal stop before pause.

34. The tense markers /È/ (realized /ÈÈ/ after a L tone) for the P tense and /É/ for the future tense tend also to remain [-low], though occasionally harmonize, the F tense morpheme apparently more readily than the P tense one. There thus seems to be vacillation between setting up these morphemes with an opaque [-LOW] specification vs. setting them up without any [LOW] autosegment.

35. The following set of pronouns used for copular and reflexive purposes, among others, apparently require an opaque [+LOW] specification:

ṁṁ	'it's me'	bɛ̀ì	'it's us'
ɔ̀ɔ̀	'it's you sg.'	bɔ̀ì	'it's you pl.'
ɛ̀ɛ̀	'it's him/her'	ɔ̀và	'it's them'

Given the forms of the plural pronouns, this [+LOW] appears to be coming from the left.

36. Actually, it has not been said yet that the only suffixes that exist in the language have the vowels /i/, /E/ and /a/. The verb bún-u 'break' appears to have a /u/ suffix. There are no /O/ suffixes, and so this logical place for vowel harmony to take place simply doesn't occur.

37. The Polish minimal pair czy 'whether' and trzy 'three' discussed by Clements and Keyser (1983) poses a potential problem, since they are acoustically distinct. Since it is the [š] part of the affricate which is longer in the case of 'three', I tentatively propose the following derivations:

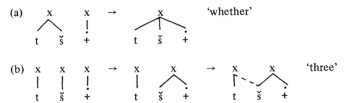

In (a) I begin, as do Clements and Keyser, with an alveo–palatal affricate, i.e. a branching x (=their C). The OCR produces the single WU in the output as seen. In (b) I begin with both the /t/ and the /š/ having their own WU. First the OCR applies, incorporating the /š/ into the same WU as the following vowel. Since this leaves behind a weighted /t/, which is low in sonority, the last stage of the derivation consists of extending the association of the /š/ to it, much as we saw in the Idoma derivation in (68b).

38. The Grassifields Bantu language Limbum, in roughly the same area as Kom, makes even more extensive use of such syllabic obstruents, e.g. ŋgv́p 'hen', ŋkfv́ 'chief', m̀bv́ 'goat', etc. Li (1984) has recently reported on similar phenomena in the Hui dialect of Chinese.

39. There are a number of interesting ramifications and further considerations that arise in this speculative account of the feature [cons]. One possibility is that the WU's and the [cons] specifications *together* form the central tier or core and that [cons] provides the anchor for other segmental features to attach to. Another possibility is that [CONS] is itself an autosegment – and hence must obey the same obligatory contour principle as tones and other autosegments. One way to arrive at this conclusion is to ask the question of what can "float", i.e. what can exist without a WU? Clearly anything which is an autosegment can have this property, e.g. a tone, a nasal feature, and vowel harmony feature, etc. We saw in my adaptation of Clements and Keyser's analysis of the h–aspiré in French in (79) that [+cons] may float. Is it possible for [+cor] or [-cont] to float? Or will we simply require [+cons] when it is a floating consonant and [-cons] when it is a floating vowel that is required (with no further feature requirements)? In this case [CONS] would have the crucial property of flotability, shared with the clear autosegments that have been set up in language after language. Finally, I would like to point out the following problem that arises if we do not establish a single feature matrix of [+cons]'s. McCarthy's (1981) representation of kátab 'he wrote' is as in (a); mine is as in (b).

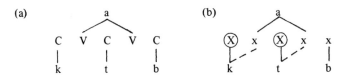

The OCR results in (b) is WU's having a [-cons] from the above tier and a [+cons] from the below tier. But which one is sequenced before which? What is clearly needed is a single place, the segmental matrices, where the [cons] features are linearized in my framework.

References

Abraham, R.C. 1951/ 1967. *The Idoma Language*. London: University of London Press.

Allen, W. Sidney. 1973. *Accent and Rhythm*. Cambridge: University Press.

Anderson, Stephen R. 1982. "The analysis of French shwa". *Language* 58.534-573.

Anderson, Stephen R. 1984. "A metrical interpretation of some traditional claims about quantity and stress". In M. Aronoff and R. Oehrle (eds.), *Language Sound Structure*, 83-106. M.I.T. Press.

Aoun, Youssef. 1979. "Is the syllable or the supersyllable a constituent?" In Safir (ed.), 95-114.

Austin, Wm. M. 1952. "A brief outline of Dagur Grammar". *Studies in Linguistics* 10.65-75.

Bird, Charles S. 1971. "Observations on initial consonant change in Southwestern Mande". In Kim, Chin-Wu and Herbert Stahlke (eds.), *Papers in African Linguistics*, 153-174. Edmonton: Linguistic Research, Inc.

Broselow, Ellen. 1976. "The phonology of Egyptian Arabic". Unpublished Ph.D. Dissertation, University of Massachusetts, Amherst.

Chomsky, Noam and Morris Halle. 1968. *The Sound Pattern of English*. New York: Harper and Row.

Clements, George N. 1980. "Akan vowel harmony: a non–linear analysis". In G.N. Clements (ed.), *Harvard Studies in Phonology* Vol. II, 108-177.

Clements, George N. 1982. "An outline of Luganda syllable structure". In William R. Leben (ed.), *Précis from the Twelfth Conference on African Linguistics*. Studies in African Linguistics, Supp. 8, 12-16.

Clements, George N. In press "Compensatory lengthening in Luganda". In Leo Wetzels and Engin Sezer (eds.), *Studies in Compensatory Lengthening*. Dordrecht: Foris.

Clements, George N. and Kevin Ford. 1979. "Kikuyu tone shift and its synchronic consequences". *Linguistic Inquiry* 10.179-210.

Clements, George N. and S. Jay Keyser. 1981. "A three–tiered theory of the syllable". *Occasional Paper No. 19*, Center for Cognitive Science, M.I.T.

Clements, George N. and S. Jay Keyser. 1983. *CV Phonology*. Cambridge, Mass.: M.I.T. Press.

Clements, George N. and Engin Sezer. 1983. "Vowel and consonant disharmony in Turkish". In Harry van der Hulst and Norval Smith (eds.), *The Structure of Phonological Representations* (Part II). Dordrecht: Foris.

De Chene, Brent Eugene. 1979. "The historical phonology of vowel length". Unpublished Ph.D. Dissertation, U.C.L.A. (Available from the I.U.L.C.)

Dwyer, David. 1974. "The historical development of Southwestern Mande consonants". Studies in African Linguistics 5.59-94.

Echeverría, Max S. and Heles Contreras. 1965. "Araucanian phonemics". I.J.A.L. 31.132-135.

George, Isaac. 1970. "Nupe tonology". *Studies in African Linguistics* 1.100-122.

Goldsmith, John. 1982. "Accent systems". In Harry van der Hulst and Norval Smith (eds.), *The Structure of Phonological Representations* (Part I), 47-63. Dordrecht: Foris.

Gudschinsky, Sarah C., Harold Popovich, and Frances Popovich. 1970. "Native reaction and phonetic similarity in Maxakalí phonology". *Language* 46.77-88.

Guerssel, Mohamed. 1978. "A condition on assimilation rules". *Linguistic Analysis* 4.225-254.

Guthrie, Malcolm. 1971. *Comparative Bantu* (Vol. II). Gregg International Publishers.

Haas, Mary R. 1977. "Tonal accent in Creek". In Larry M. Hyman (ed.), *Studies in Stress and Accent*. 195-208. Southern California Occassional Papers in Linguistics No. 4.

Hale, Kenneth. 1973. "Deep-surface canonical disparities in relation to analysis and change: an Australian example". In Thomas A. Sebeok (ed.), *Current Trends in Linguistics* Vol. 11, 401-458.

Halle, Morris and Jean-Roger Vergnaud. 1980. "Three-dimensional phonology". Journal of Linguistic Research 1.83-105.

Haraguchi, Shosuke. 1977. *The Tone Pattern of Japanese: an Autosegmental Theory of Tonology*. Tokyo: Kaitakusha.

Hayes, Bruce. 1981. "A metrical theory of stress rules". Unpublished Ph.D. Dissertation, M.I.T. (Available from I.U.L.C.)

Hohepa, Patrick W. 1967. *A Profile Generative Grammar of Maori*. I.J.A.L. Memoir 20.

Holmer, Nils M. 1947. *Critical and Comparative Grammar of the Cuna Language*. Göteborg.

Holmer, Nils M. 1949. "Goajiro (Arawak) I: phonology". I.J.A.L. 15. 45-56.

Howard, Irwin. 1972. "A directional theory of rule application in phonology". Unpublished Ph.D. Dissertation, M.I.T. (Available from I.U.L.C.)

Hyman, Larry M. 1970a. "How concrete is phonology?" Language 46.58-76.

Hyman, Larry M. 1970b. "The role of borrowing in the justification of phonological grammars". *Studies in African Linguistics* 1.1-48.

Hyman, Larry M. 1972. *A Phonological Study of Fe?fe?-Bamileke*. Studies in African Linguistics, Supp. 4.

Hyman, Larry M. 1973a. "Notes on the history of Southwestern Mande". *Studies in African Linguistics* 4.183-196

Hyman, Larry M. 1973b. "The role of consonant types in natural tonal assimilations". In Larry M. Hyman (ed.), *Consonant Types and Tone*, 151-179. *Southern California Occasional Papers in Linguistics* No. 1.

Hyman, Larry M. 1975. *Phonology: Theory and Analysis*. New York: Holt, Rinehart and Winston.

Hyman, Larry M. 1976. "Phonologization". In Alphonse Juilland (ed.), *Linguistic Studies Offered to Joseph H. Greenberg*, Vol. 2, 407-418. Saratoga, CA: Anma Libri.

Hyman, Larry M. 1977. "On the nature of linguistic stress". In Larry M. Hyman (ed.), *Studies in Stress and Accent*, 37-82. *Southern California Occasional Papers in Linguistics* No. 4.

Hyman, Larry M. 1978. "Tone and/or accent". In Donna Jo Napoli (ed.), *Elements of Tone, Stress and Intonation*, 1-20. Georgetown University.

Hyman, Larry M. (ed.), 1979. *Aghem Grammatical Structure. Southern California Occasional Papers in Linguistics* No. 7.

Hyman, Larry M. 1980. "Tonal accent in Somali". *Studies in African Linguistics* 12.169-203.

Hyman, Larry M. 1982a. "The representation of length in Gokana". In *Proceedings of the First Annual West Coast Conference on Formal Linguistics*, 198-206. Stanford University.

Hyman, Larry M. 1982b. "The representation of nasality in Gokana". In Harry van der Hulst and Norval Smith (eds.), *The Structure of Phonological Representations* (Part I), 111-130. Dordrecht: Foris.

Hyman, Larry M. 1983a. "Are there syllables in Gokana?" In Jonathan Kaye et al. (eds.), *Current Issues in African Linguistics* (vol. 2), 171-179. Dordrecht: Foris.

Hyman, Larry M. 1983b. "Globality and the accentual analysis of Luganda tone". *Journal of Linguistic Research*, 4.1-40.

Hyman, Larry M. 1984. "On the weightlessness of syllable onsets". In *Proceedings of the 10th Annual Berkeley Linguistic Society Meeting*.

Hyman, Larry M. and Ernest Rugwa Byarushengo. 1983. "A model of Haya tonology". In George N. Clements and John Goldsmith (eds.), *Autosegmental Studies in Bantu Tone*. Dordrecht: Foris.

Hyman, Larry M. and Bernard Comrie. 1981. "Logophoric reference in Gokana". *Journal of African Languages and Linguistics* 3.19-37.

Hyman, Larry M. and Russell G. Schuh. 1974. "Universals of tone rules: evidence from West Africa". *Linguistic Inquiry* 5.81-115.

Jakobson, Roman. 1931. "Die Betonung und ihre Rolle in der Word- und Syntagmaphonologie". *Travaux du Cercle Linguistique de Prague* IV. Reprinted in *Roman Jakobson, Selected Writings* I, 117-136. The Hague: Mouton.

Jakobson, Roman. 1937. "Über die Beschaffenheit der prosodischen Gegensätze". In *Roman Jakobson, Selected Writings* I, 254-261. The Hague: Mouton.

Kaye, Jonathan D. 1981. "Les diphthongues cachées du vata". *Studies in African Linguistics* 12.225-244.

Kaye, Jonathan D. 1982. "Implosives as liquids". In William R. Leben (ed.), *Précis from the 12th Conference on African Linguistics*, 78-81. *Studies in African Linguistics*, Supp. 8.

Kaye, Jonathan D. and Jean Lowenstamm. 1981. "Syllable structure and markedness theory". In A. Belletti et al. (eds.), *Theory of Markedness in Generative Grammar* 287-316. Pisa.

Kenstowicz, Michael. 1970 "On the notation of vowel length in Lithuanian". *Papers in Linguistics* 3.73-113.

Kenstowicz, Michael. 1982. "Gemination and spirantization in Tigrinya". *Studies in the Linguistic Sciences*, 12.103-122.

Kiparsky, Paul. 1973. "'Elsewhere' in phonology". In Stephen R. Anderson and Paul Kiparsky (eds.), *A Festschrift for Morris Halle*, 93-106. New York: Holt, Rinehart and Winston.

Kiparsky, Paul. 1979, "Metrical structure assignment is cyclic". *Linguistic Inquiry* 10.421-441.

Kiparsky, Paul. 1982. "Lexical morphology and phonology". In I.-S. Yang (ed.), *Linguistics in the Morning Calm*. Seoul: Hanshin.

Kisseberth, Charles W. 1984. "Digo tonology". In George N. Clements and John Goldsmith (eds.), *Autosegmental Studies in Bantu Tone*. Dordrecht: Foris.

Kisseberth, Charles W. and Mohammad I. Abasheikh. 1974. "Vowel length in Chi-Mwi:ni- - a case study of the role of grammar in phonology. In *Natural Phonology Parasession*. Chicago Linguistic Society.

Krueger, John R. 1961. *Chuvash Manual.* Indiana University Publication No. 7 in the Uralic and Altaic Series.

Ladefoged, Peter, 1971. *Preliminaries to Linguistic Phonetics.* Chicago: University of Chicago Press.

Larsen, Raymond S. and Eunice Victoria Pike. 1949. "Huasteco intonations and phonemes". *Language* 25.268-277.

Leben, William R. 1973. "Suprasegmental phonology". (M.I.T. Ph.D Dissertation available from Garland Press.)

Leben, William R. 1974. "Rule inversion in Chadic: a reply". *Studies in African Linguistics,* 5.265-278.

Leben, William R. 1976a. "The tones of English intonation". *Linguistic Analysis* 2.69-107.

Leben, William R. 1976b. "Doubling and reduplication in Hausa plurals". In Alphons Juilland (ed.), *Linguistic Studies Offered to Joseph H. Greenberg.* Saratoga, CA: Anma Libri.

Leben, William R. 1977. "Parsing Hausa plurals". In P. Newman and R.M. Newman (eds.), *Papers in Chadic Linguistics.* Leiden: Africa–Studiecentrum.

Leben, William R. 1978. "The representation of tone". In Victoria A. Fromkin (ed.), *Tone: A Linguistic Survey,* 177-220. New York: Academic Press.

Leben, William R. 1980. "A metrical analysis of length". *Linguistic Inquiry* 11.497-509.

Levin, Juliette. 1983. "Reduplication and prosodic structure". Ms., M.I.T.

Li, Charles N. 1984. "From verb–medial analytic language to verb–final synthetic language: the Hui language of Western China". Paper presented at the 10th Annual Berkely Linguistic Society Meeting.

Liberman, Mark and Alan Prince. 1977. "On stress and linguistic rhythm". Linguistic Inquiry 8.249-336.

Lieber, Rochelle, 1983. "New developments in autosegmental morphology: consonant mutation". In proceedings of the Second Annual West Coast Conference on Formal Linguistics, 165-175. Stanford University.

Lieber, Rochelle. 1984. "Consonant gradation in Fula: an autosegmental approach". In Mark Aronoff and Richard T. Oehrle (ed.), *Language Sound Structure,* 329-345. M.I.T. Press.

Lindskog, John N. and Ruth M. Brend. 1962. "Cayapa phonemics". In *Ecuadorian Indian Language* I, 31-44. S.I.L.

Lowenstamm, Jean. 1981. "On the maximal cluster approach to syllable structure". *Linguistic Inquiry* 12.575-604.

Maddieson, Ian. 1970. "The inventory of features". In I. Maddieson (ed.), *Tone in Generative Phonology,* 3-18. *Research Notes,* Vol. 3, Parts 2 &3, Department of Linguistics and Nigerian Languages, University of Ibadan, Nigeria.

Mannessy, Gabriel. 1964. "L'alternance consonantique en kpelle, manya, bandi et loma". *Journal of African Languages* 3.162-178.

Marantz, Alec. 1982, "Re–reduplication", *Linguistic Inquiry* 13.435-482.

Martin, Samuel E. 1961. *Dagur Mongolian Grammar, Texts and Lexicon.* Indiana University Publications in Uralic and Altaic Series, Vol. 4.

McCarthy, John J. 1979. "Formal problems in Semitic phonology and morphology". Unpublished Ph.D. Dissertation, M.I.T. (Available from I.U.L.C.)

McCarthy, John J. 1981. "A prosodic theory of nonconcatenative morphology". *Linguistic Inquiry* 12.373-418.

McCarthy, John J. 1983a. "The verbal system of Chaha (Central Western Gurage)". Draft of *Formal Morphology,* Chapter 4, Section 2.

McCarthy, John J. 1983b. "Morpheme form and phonological representation". Paper presented at Sloan Conference on Hierarchy and Constituency in Phonology. University of Massachusetts, Amherst, April 30, 1983.

McCawley, James D. 1968. *The Phonological Component of a Grammar of Japanese.* Monographs on Linguistic Analysis 2. The Hague: Mouton.

McCawley, James D. 1977. "Accent in Japanese". In Larry M. Hyman (ed.), *Studies in Stress and Accent*, 261-302. *Southern California Occasional Papers in Linguistics* No. 4.

McLaughren, Mary. 1984. "Autosegmental account of tone in Zulu". In George N. Clements and John Goldsmith (eds.), *Autosegmental Studies in Bantu Tone.* Dordrecht: Foris.

Meeussen, A.E. 1963. "Morphotonology of the Tonga verb". *Journal of African Languages*, 72-92.

Meeussen, A.E. 1965. "A note on permutation in Kpelle-Mende". *African Language Studies* 6.112-116.

Mohanan, K.P. 1979. "On syllabicity". In Safir (1979b), 182-190.

Mohanan, K.P. 1981. "Lexical phonology". Unpublished Ph. D. Dissertation, M.I.T.

Newman, Paul. 1972. "Syllable weight as a phonological variable". *Studies in African Linguistics* 3.301-323.

Newman, Paul and Bello Ahmad Salim. 1981. "Hausa dipthongs". *Lingua* 55.101-121.

Odden, David. n.d. "A nonlinear approach to vowel length in Kimatuumbi". Ms. University of Illinois.

Odden, David. 1982. "Tonal phenomena in Kishambaa". *Studies in African Linguistics*, 13.177-208.

Ohsiek, Deborah. 1976. "Heavy syllables and stress". In Alan Bell and Joan B. Hooper (eds.), *Syllables and Segments*, 35-43. Amsterdam: North-Holland.

Penchoen, Thomas G. 1973, *Tamazight of the Ayt Ndhir. Afroasiatic Dialects*, Vol. 1. Los Angeles: Undena Publications.

Pesetsky, David. 1979. "Russian morphology and lexical theory". Ms. M.I.T.

Pike Eunice V. 1974. "A multiple stress system versus a tone system". I.J.A.L. 40.169-175.

Pike, Kenneth L. and Eunice V. Pike. 1947. "Immediate constituents of Mazateco syllables". I.J.A.L. 13.78-91.

Poppe, Nikolaus. 1951. *Khalkha-Mongolische Grammatik*. Wiesbaden: Franz Steiner Verlag, GMBH.

Prince, Alan S. 1980. "A metrical theory for Estonian quantity". *Linguistic Inquiry* 11.511-562.

Pulleyblank, Douglas. 1983. *Tone in Lexical Phonology*. Unpublished Ph.D. Dissertation, M.I.T. To appear, Reidel Press.

Rialland, Annie. In Press. "Schwa et syllabe en français". In Leo Wetzels and Engin Sezer (eds.), *Studies in Compensatory Lengthening*. Dordrecht: Foris.

Safir, Ken. 1979a. "Metrical structure in Capanahua". In Ken Safir (1979b), *Papers on Syllable Structure, Metrical Structure and Harmony Processes*, 95-114. *M.I.T. Working Papers in Linguistics* Vol. 1.

Sapir, Edward and Morris Swadesh. 1960. *Yana Dictionary*. University of California Publications in Linguistics No. 22.

Saib, Jilali. 1976a. "A phonological study of Tamazight Berber: dialect of the Ayt Ndhir". Unpublished Ph.D. Dissertation, U.C.L.A.

Saib, Jilali. 1976b. "Segment organization and the syllable in Tamazight Berber". In Alan Bell and Joan B. Hooper (eds.), *Syllables and Segments*, 93-104. Amsterdam: North Holland.

Schane, Sanford A. 1968. *French Phonology and Morphology*. Cambridge, Mass.: M.I.T. Press.

Schuh, Russell G. 1972. "Rule inversion in Chadic". *Studies in African Linguistics* 3.379-398.

Selkirk, Elizabeth O. 1980. "The role of prosodic categories in English word stress". *Linguistic Inquiry* 11.563–605.

Smith, N.V. 1967. "The phonology of Nupe". *Journal of African Languages* 6.153-169.

Steriade, Donca. 1982. "Greek prosodies and the nature of syllabification". Unpublished Ph.D. dissertation, M.I.T.

Steriade, Donca. 1983. "Relative sonority scales". Paper presented at the Second Annual West Coast Conference on Formal Linguistics.

Steriade, Donca. 1984. "Rumanian syllable structure". Paper presented at 10th Annual Berkely Linguistic Society Meeting.

Swadesh, Morris. 1946. "Chitimacha". *Linguistic Structures of Native America*, No. 6, 312-336.

Taylor, Douglas. 1954. "Phonemes of the Hopkins (British Honduras) dialect of Island Carib". I.J.A.L. 21.233-241.

Tranel, Bernard. 1981. *Concreteness in Generative Phonology*. Berkeley: University of California Press.

Trubetzkoy, N. 1939/1969. *Principles of Phonology* (translated by Christiane A.M. Baltaxe). Berkeley and Los Angeles: University of California Press.

Trutenau, H.M.J. 1972. "Synchronic/diachronic variation of the type $/CV_1lV_1/ \sim /ClV_1/$ in the Ga language". *Proceedings of the Seventh* International Congress of Phonetic Sciences, Montreal. The Hague: Mouton. 618-622.

Vago, Robert M. 1980. *The Sound Pattern of Hungarian*. Benjamins.

Welmers, William E. 1962. "The phonology of Kpelle". *Journal of African Languages* 1.69-93.

Welmers, William E. 1969. "The morphology of Kpelle nominals". *Journal of African Languages* 8.73-101.

Zide, Norman H. 1965. "Gutob–Remo vocalism and glottalised vowels in Proto–Munda". *Lingua* 4.43-53.